Caring Liturgies

Caring Liturgies

The Pastoral Power of Christian Ritual

SUSAN MARIE SMITH

Fortress Press

Minneapolis

CARING LITURGIES
The Pastoral Power of Christian Ritual

Cover design: Tory Herman
Cover images © iStockphoto.com/Chepko Daril; © iStockphoto.com/Dirk Rietschel
Book design: PerfecType, Nashville, TN

Library of Congress Cataloging-in-Publication Data is available
ISBN 978-0-8006-9736-5

Manufactured in the U.S.A.
16 15 14 13 12 1 2 3 4 5 6 7 8 9 10

Contents

Acknowledgments

🦜 It takes a village to raise a child and to midwife a book. The community, care, and critique of others brought this book into being.

I give thanks for all who shared their liturgical labor with me: Miriam, Sharon, Paula, Gayle, Stephanie, Trish, Amy, Justin, Josy, Anamonica, Betsy, Dennie, Wendy, Cat, Nancy and Carrie-on, Margaret, Julie, the Fischer family, Tom, David, Jim and Frederick, S. Moya, Heath, Karen, Erin, Janiece, Kinga Reka, Brigitte, Mary, S. Mary Jo, S. Therese, and S. Annie, Marlene, and the S. Women in Ministry, among others.

Many stories could not find a place in the limited space of this book, so I include several on my blog, WalkingtheWay.org, along with a bibliography.

The women who created rites for me gave me inside experience of ritual power and possibility: Judy, Paula, Gayle, Mary, Josy, Grailville and company; Judith, Jan, Nancy, Barbara, Jen and company; Lucia, Kristen, Suzan, Barbara, Mo, Jane, Kate, and Julia; and the Sisters of the Order of St. Benedict who invited me to dance in their liturgy. Men know about ritualization, too, and I give thanks for the rites prepared by Logan, Larry, Robert, Hal, and Art, with Vallory and the UM Order of St. Luke.

Many read early parts of the manuscript and gave invaluable input. Thanks to the first group: Jack Dickson, Anne Hutcherson, Teresa Stewart, SueEllen McCalley, and Nancy Pauls. Other blessed readers include Bill Doggett, Jason Lewis, Richard Fitzgerald, Jim Gordon, Angie Loomis, Amanda Ross, Kathy Todd, Lisa Senuta, Robert Martin, Jim Hempler, Laura Simmons, Nelvin Vos, and Frank Henderson. Gayle Reichert, whose poem appears herein, gave up a summer to read and respond to chapters. Mary McGann, writing partner for years, talked and prayed me through myriad revisions.

Several others also prayed this book into being: my sister Carol, Diane, Bill and Catherine, Sue Ellen, Nancy, Amy, Jude, Lucia, and Rosemary; and from the next world, Mari Koch. Others were hospitable nurturers: S. Annie, Mother Anne, Cornelia, neighbor Betsy, jogging partner Linda, cousin Dennis, my oblate group, Lea Durard, Devena Reed, Jerry and Randi Walker, Mary McGann, RSCJ, and Mary Dian and Warren Molton.

Former students, especially Khenneth, Kyle, Kathy, and Meg, and my exceptional student assistants, Kim Dominic and Cathryn Love, were invaluable.

Thank you to my blessed writing coaches: Dorothy Duff Brown, Nancy Barry, and Bill Tammeus. David Schlafer and Marvin Anderson are encouragers par excellence. My editor David Lott is a godsend.

Dean Judith Berling of the Graduate Theological Union granted me a visiting professorship to work in the GTU library. St. Paul School of Theology granted me a sabbatical, and the Collegeville Institute of Ecumenical and Cultural Research at St. John's University, Minnesota, a place to write and colleagues in conversation. A Wabash Center research grant enabled me to pursue new veins of research.

To my mentors I give deepest thanks: Louis Weil, Michael Aune, Duncan Ferguson, James Fowler, Don Saliers, S. Mary Collins, Peggy Skelton, and Catherine Bell, whose too early death is a loss to all who study ritual. To her and to my Aunt Margot, in whose home I completed these pages, I dedicate this volume.

Worship as Ritual

Understanding and Claiming Ethical Christian Ritual

What can I do? My wife just had a miscarriage—it was to have been our first baby. She is disconsolate and we both feel so alone. I love her so much, and I would do anything to comfort her! Isn't there something I could do to help her? Doesn't the church have some kind of ritual to help me love her and comfort her in this terrible time?

Pastor, something has changed in me. I'm turning my life over—I'm going to give it to God in the church. I'm not sure what kind of ministry I'm called to, but whatever it is, that's what I'm going to do. Could we celebrate this in some way? I want my family of faith to know this, to witness my commitment, to pray for me.

I just don't understand it. The preacher says that Christianity is "a way of life" of loving all people, of justice and mercy, of reconciliation. We're to love the Lord with all our heart, soul, mind and strength. But when the folks in this church try to do that for real, we get little spiritual support. For instance, we do a bang-up job on weddings, but when the honeymoon is over, these new couples are left to fend for themselves, with the congregation doing nothing more to nurture and sustain them through their continuing milestones and struggles. The one thing churches ought to know how to do is celebrate what God is doing in our midst. Can't we do better than this?

What Is "Ritual"?

Christians care deeply about their worship, but many would be dismayed to hear that worship is an instance of the broadly human practice called "ritual," because the word *ritual* has mixed connotations, some of which are infelicitous. For some, it implies meaningless, incomprehensible, or rote action: "empty" ritual. In psychology, it is associated with certain pathologically patterned behaviors, such as Lady MacBeth washing her hands repeatedly. It also functions as a technical liturgical term referring specifically to the words said (and not the actions done) when Christians gather for Sunday Mass. Anthropologists study an indigenous culture's rituals in order to understand their beliefs, values, and kinship relations.

In 1972, however, anthropologist Ronald Grimes invited religious scholars to rethink what the study of ritual could reveal not only about other cultures' religions but also about our own. Grimes opened up a new way to study Christian and Jewish worship by approaching it the way anthropologists have approached primitive cultures' worship: in its enactment, seeking to learn what it might reveal about beliefs, values, and relationships. Grimes' seminal work in the then-new field called "ritual studies" led Jews and Christians to view worship more humbly, as practices that are part of the broader human category of ritual.[1]

Grimes was interested not only in common rituals of various religions, but was aware of the numinous aspect of certain behaviors that may not be officially sanctioned by an authorized religious or denominational group. For example, "liturgy" implies a worship service with a repeated structure. Then what does one call a rite that may be done only once? If "worship" implies what Christians do together on Sundays, then what does one call a devotional gathering, perhaps in a home, perhaps on a Tuesday? What about rites that may not be public worship but, rather, private and confidential? Further, would there be ways to study Christian or Jewish worship with some ideological distance, just as one would study worship in, say, an indigenous Samoan setting? For this to happen, it became necessary to give up earlier prejudicial thinking that Christian worship is its own category, and instead, to study worship as an instance of something all human cultures do: ritual.

This book draws upon ritual studies, along with liturgical theology, to offer principles for the making of rites that could respond to the needs expressed in the opening anecdotes: rites of transition and healing that may be one-time events particular to a person, a congregation, or a situation. To provide the ritual basis for these principles, I begin with a synopsis of some insights from ritual studies, to show not only how ritual works in general, but also why it is important that Christians learn principles of worship making, both for more insightful planning and leading of Sunday worship, and here especially for generating occasional and pastoral rituals when it will help the baptized toward healing or transition.

Before doing this, however, it is important to note two kinds of "bad ritual." First, *rites can be death dealing*. Rite makers must be concerned about unethical ritual, that is, rituals that manifest an ethic which does not free or which fails to proclaim or mediate life to all. Ritual is powerful, both for good or for ill. Positively, it can gather the community in a structure strong enough to hold many people, conflicting points of view, and varied emotions together in unity. It can be engaged to empower and heal participants, and to release and redeem them from the stranglehold of emotional, psychological, or spiritual oppression. Life-giving ritual can create unity out of estrangement, support out of isolation, and hope out of fear or despair. But ritual power also can be engaged to oppress persons or to manipulate them toward that which violates their best interest or even the common good. One thinks of the rituals of the Third Reich in Germany, which turned moral people against fellow Germans who were Gypsies, Jews, homosexuals, or deemed mentally deficient. But dog-fighting rings or family rituals where dysfunction is perpetrated upon the vulnerable are other examples of unethical ritual. The ritual maker's morality, intention, and competence are primary in assuring that rituals are freeing, life giving, and redemptive.

Second, *rites can be meaningless*, referring to nothing. Rite leaders must be concerned about rote, stodgy, or disconnected ritual that can actually impede worshipers' connection with the holy. Many worship leaders as well as worshipers "go through the motions," even on a Sunday morning, and never open themselves to the Spirit of God, notice other worshipers, allow the prayers and songs and Scripture to touch one's own heart and soul, or make connections with real life. We have all experienced worship leaders whose bodies and words were present, but their minds and hearts somewhere else entirely. This is neither good worship nor good leadership.

This book is written for those who care about making ethical, life-giving rites that are alive with an integrity which connects mind and heart, body and spirit, people with each other, worshipers with the leader, and congregations with God. I assume that those who claim the sacred trust to mediate rites of healing or transition understand that *how* they plan and lead is often as important as *what* they plan and lead, and that they surround their planning and their leading with prayer for the presence and guidance of God's Holy Spirit. One's own morality, ritual intention and competence, and care for siblings in the faith are essential.[2] The best way to assure one does not fall into leading or participating in either unethical or prosaic ritual is to learn its grammar and its poetry, which is what this book seeks to offer.

Further, ritual expresses a story. Here, our point of reference is the Christian story, which is fundamentally life giving, freeing, and redemptive and calls people to be selflessly loving. The six principles offered herein rely upon morality and life-giving intention to guide their use. This book assumes that persons with self-knowledge, who have grown to a level of maturity so as to distinguish between their own needs and opinions and those of the ones they serve, and who have a heart for the healing and growth of the people of God, will put these principles to use.

The particular focus of this book is *ritual competence.* By that I mean both intellectual understanding and reflective practice in planning and leading ritual that expresses and engenders Christian ethics, meaning, and structures, as well as in "reading" the meaning of rites as they are mediated to the worshipers. Ritual competence in a Christian context includes practice in and intention toward embodying Christian ethics, the Christian story, and Christian symbols.

Four Attributes of Ritual Practice

A breakthrough in the field of ritual studies occurred in 1992 when Catherine Bell, a scholar of the history of religions, published her seminal book *Ritual Theory, Ritual Practice,*[3] in which she distinguished the study of theory from the study of practice, and thereby opened up the study of ritual by focusing on describing rather than defining ritual. According to Bell, ritual accomplishes that which cannot be accomplished in any other way.[4] Ritual is not a "thing" but, rather, a *way of doing* things. Bell identifies four attributes of ritual as practice that are profoundly helpful for understanding any ritual, including worship, liturgy, and particular rites of healing and transition: (1) ritual creates strategic contrast; (2) it is contextual or situational; (3) it operates beneath the level of consciousness; and (4) it shifts and mediates power. Understanding these is the first step in developing ritual fluency and competence.

1. *Ritual creates strategic contrast,* which is to say that it is a strategy for distinguishing and thus privileging one event (the ritual event) from regular events in order to accomplish something. A birthday party may have the same family around the same table with the same pattern of food and dessert as any other meal. But for *this* dinner, Billy gets to pick the menu and eat off the special birthday plate, because it's *his birthday.* The napkins say "Happy Birthday," and the centerpiece is a cake with Billy's name on it and six candles. But after dinner, before the cake is cut, presents appear from nowhere. Billy enjoys unwrapping them and seeing what is given to him—just for being Billy, for being alive, for having lived six years. People know what to do: they smile, they are glad or enthusiastic, they appreciate the gifts along with Billy and on his behalf. Then, at last, the cake is moved to Billy's place, everyone stands, the lights are dimmed, the candles lit, and everyone sings "Happy Birthday to You" as his face radiates joy. He makes a wish, blows out the candles, everyone cheers. The cake is cut and served. And Billy does not have to help with dishes on this night. Thus, with a few strategic modifications, a family meal is turned into a celebration of Billy that he will never forget.

Similarly, a church might strategically modify its regular Sunday service to send people off as they move to a new town. The family may be called before the congregation during the prayer time; the change is announced; the congregation sings a blessing song; prayer is offered on their behalf. Following the service, there may even be a reception for them. This is a simple strategic variation on the normal rite by which something important is accomplished: a celebration and thanksgiving for this family and sending them off with love and blessing.

Good rituals have the right balance of continuity with the ordinary (such as a family dinner, Sunday worship) and contrast from the ordinary (for example, birthday cake and gifts, farewell prayers and blessings). Without enough "symbolic rupture"[5] or contrast, ritual will not hold enough power to effect change. With too much contrast or symbolic rupture, the particular worshipers will not be able to relate to or understand the event. To make holy, one sets apart. Ritual is a way of using strategies to set apart, to alter the every day to make one moment, one instance of an event, special, singled out, and holy, so that it matters and is memorable. Ritual, then, strategically establishes a contrast that privileges one moment over other similar moments, making it special, meaningful, and holy.[6]

2. *Ritual is situational.* Besides its strategic aspect, ritual has a "grassroots" aspect. It is not an unchangeable "thing" that a person could carry or give to others, the way one might take a box of chocolates or a bouquet of flowers to the houses of dinner hosts over the years. Instead, ritual is a practice that arises out of a situation. Jesus, for example, used the occasion of the Passover meal (according to Matthew, Mark, and Luke) to communicate something important to his disciples about what was going to happen to him, and how they could be with him as often as they would "do this, in remembrance" of him. In one house blessing, it was an important symbol to light a fire in the fireplace, both as warmth of the hearth and hospitality of the home, but also for the owner to truly claim the house that had felt borrowed, since in eight years of residing there, the fireplace had never been lit.

In another example, a pastoral colleague began meeting regularly with a gentleman in long-term care who had cancer. He loved to smoke cigars, and since she did, too, they smoked together on each visit. It was a bonding time of communion between them as they smoked and talked, and she listened to stories of his life. One day she sensed that he was approaching death, and he offered her one of his very expensive Cuban cigars. She asked if she could not smoke it that day. Instead, they talked and prayed about this life and the next, and completed all that needed to be done. At the man's funeral, the pastor got up to preach the sermon, lit the Cuban cigar, and proceeded to tell his story while she smoked, shared their relationship, and made the connection with the Holy Spirit who fills and connects, abundantly. While she knew that smoking a cigar from the pulpit would usually be utterly inappropriate, here it signified this man's loves (smoking, friendship) and reinforced the sermon message, which focused on the unexpected ways in which God makes communion among us in extravagant and holy ways. There were tears at the funeral that day because the sermon made real the truth of this beloved man's particular quirky individuality and the way he connected to people. Ritual arises out of and fits a particular situation.

3. *Ritual operates below the level of conscious awareness.* Paul Tillich notes that a symbol "opens up levels of reality which otherwise are closed for us" and also "opens up hidden depths of our own being."[7] But when a

person recognizes how a symbol is operating, its effectiveness ceases. Bell borrows the term *misrecognition*[8] to express the fact that ritual works as long as its working is not recognized. Rituals are effective inasmuch as people can enter into their energy and movement and be carried along by the flow. But if ritual calls attention to itself, the flow is broken, and so is the power. Watching a ballet where fairies seem to fly through the air is mesmerizing, but if attention should follow the wires lifting them to a red-faced, sweating pulley operator above the stage, the light-hearted effect of flying on stage is now lost. Or if the whole congregation is very present to the Holy Spirit who is palpably among them, and the preacher inserts a five-minute explanation of the worship or tells a joke or otherwise draws attention to herself, suddenly attention will be wrested from the Holy Spirit.

In contrast, it is also possible to intentionally hold focus on the ritual action unfolding and avoid distraction. For example, *Godly Play,* a children's curriculum based upon the Montessori method of children's education, teaches a particular way to tell stories that enables the children to keep focused. Teachers are taught that when they tell a story with the children in a circle around them, they should keep their minds *and their eyes* on the story props, and the children always follow suit. During the story telling, the teachers never look at or address the children nor ask questions until after the story is told. Rather, by keeping their own total focus on the story, the children are able to be single-minded in their attention, which is never broken. There is no distraction that would draw attention to the storyteller or the room or the hour or how each other is responding. In this way, they enter the story and become part of it.[9] The same approach is suggested for lectors and others who proclaim the Scripture story in worship.[10]

What is effective about symbols and rituals is that they invoke a higher reality or "world" into which participants are invited. This aspect of ritual is liberating, because participants are freed to enter a realm greater than themselves. They can "lose themselves" and are enabled to surrender to and be part of something over which they are not in charge. At the same time, this aspect of ritual places a responsibility on the ritual maker to be trustworthy, to hold the bounds of the container or "world," and thus not to be too casual about the rite. There is a sacred trust in inviting persons into a ritual setting in which they are free to be vulnerable without being afraid. For participants to receive and engage the

ritual action unself-consciously, ritual leaders need the ritual ethics, fluency, and competence to focus completely on the present moment and on the ritual event as it unfolds.
4. *Ritual shifts and mediates power.* Ritual exercises what Bell calls *redemptive hegemony*: it rearranges power and authority in redemptive, healing, life-giving ways.[11] In ritual, power can be moved, increased, or decreased. Thus those who have been victims and felt powerless can come away from a ritual literally empowered. Hierarchical power understood at the beginning of a ritual can, depending upon how ritual factors are engaged (for example, community, metaphor and symbol, honesty, sacrifice), be strengthened, lessened, or rearranged.

The goal of honest and ethical ritual makers is to engender rituals that will mediate God's power redemptively. To enable God's power requires avoiding ego power. This is helped by attending to Christian theology, committing to Christian ethics, practicing one's own prayer, self-purification, and self-care, and desiring care of the person the ritual is for, called the "focal person."[12] Rite makers seek to match their intention with God's intention for the focal person: hope, truth, freedom, mercy, justice, love—abundant life. While any honest ritual maker will want these things "in general," this is not enough: one must be vigilant and intentional before the rite about imagining and removing any barriers to mediating the full life Christ would want for the participants.

For example, a woman who has been victimized by her family may feel and believe she is utterly powerless, and may renege on making any decisions for her own well-being. One hopes she will find her way to psychotherapy to learn the causes and symptoms of disempowerment and patterns of reempowerment. Understanding may be the first step so that her will to change may be engaged and the healing process started. But understanding alone may be inadequate to enable her actually to change the patterns that lead her to seek disempowering relationships. For this, a ritual is often most effective, for in ritual action, power shifts. Power can be gained and given. Knowing this, paying attention to how power is shifted redemptively in rituals, and practicing with others ways of enabling proper empowerment to happen in ritual is the work of the churches and the work of any competent ritual maker. Because rituals well done are so potent, it behooves us as ritual designers and leaders to be aware of our power. It is a sacred trust to mediate the mystery of God's power through this form of worship.

These four attributes are basic to all ritual, extremely helpful in understanding how worship works, and valuable for persons seeking ritual fluency and competence. Understanding them can help worship leaders and pastors make worship more effective, life giving, empowering, and healing, as well as avoid inadvertent flaws that could render the worship they lead ineffective at best, or harmful at worst. Building on these four descriptions of how ritual works, then, it is possible to understand why churches ought to intentionally offer caring ritual.

Reasons to Create Caring Liturgies

Arising out of Catherine Bell's seminal insights, there are five reasons the churches ought to invest in making rituals for all the baptized for their growth into God and the fulfillment of their ministries.

1. *Rituals are needed to enable human growth and maturity.* Many churches have not put a priority on intentionally calling and enabling their people to mature—spiritually, psychologically, socially, and intellectually—for the sake of their identity in Christ and their service to the world. Many churches want to grow in numbers of attendees, but are less concerned with those persons' growth in commitment. They too often fail to consider how their programs enable parishioners to mature fully as persons, following Jesus in becoming fully human. Calling the churches to draw upon their liturgical traditions to make rituals for the sake of Christian growth and maturity is a call for intentional energy to be spent on enabling the baptized to grow in Christ.

Theologian William Bouwsma has shown two models of adulthood that exist side by side in the Christian tradition. One asserts that growth is essential to the Christian life (adulthood). The other assumes that stability is better than change so that growth is not so important (manhood). In other words, churches that have failed to support growth among all the baptized may have followed the second without realizing that the first is also part of the tradition. And in centuries when Christianity was the dominant religion, maturity only for the clergy was emphasized. But now, it is imperative among post-Christendom Christian leaders to reexamine the importance of investing in mature personhood among the baptized, and therefore making rituals for them.[13]

The idea that churches should intentionally engage in developing sound, sensitive, and competent rituals to enable the baptized to grow into Christ arises out of the understanding that humans are called to fulfill the potential God has given them. Growth and becoming are foundationally biblical. Growth—sanctification—is an antidote to sin. The apostles said to Jesus, "Increase our faith" (Luke 17:5). It is the churches' work to help enable people to mature in faith,[14] especially those who are covenanted to Christ in baptism. At whatever age people are baptized, baptism into Christ is not the culmination of their faith life, but a new beginning. If the church has an interest in growing Christians, then the church is not finished once they've emerged from the baptismal waters. Rather, the baptized, united with Christ in his death and resurrection and now part of his body, are committed to growing into the mind of Christ (Phil. 2:5), to be like him (Phil. 3:10), becoming a holy nation (1 Pet. 2:9), going on to perfection or maturity (Heb. 6:1). Baptism initiates into participation in the divine life (2 Pet. 1:4), being changed into the likeness of Christ (2 Cor. 3:17-18), growing from being children of God (Irenaeus) to being adults of God to becoming God-like.[15] Once baptized, Christians are compelled to grow and mature in Christ. Alongside congregational worship, personal Christian ritual is an important part of any Christian growth, ongoing conversion, and change, and is a primary gift the churches have to offer.

2. *Rituals are needed to help people through many and particular times of suffering and times of transition.* Every mammal changes. It's built right into our biogenetic make-up: birth, puberty, reproduction, death. But for humans, biologic changes are interpreted by cultural meanings through rites of passage at these four stages. Church culture has superimposed its own meanings, commonly experienced at marriages and funerals, but also at other significant passages beyond the four biogenetic ones; for instance, profession to monastic life, sending forth on a pilgrimage, ordination, or enthroning a Christian monarch.

Now is the era for extending the availability of church rites of healing and passage beyond exceptional Christians to all the baptized, and for pastorally acknowledging life crises when members of Christ's body encounter dire moments on their journey toward closer Christ-likeness. At such moments of dangerous opportunity, persons are vulnerable. They need help.

Coping with life crises is like walking a path and suddenly coming to a lake or river with no way across or finding your way blocked by a long wall or fence. To keep going, you need help. At the lake, you need a boat to carry you across. At the fence, you need some way to climb over. Ritual can be the ferry, the ladder, or stile carrying you from the stuck or stranded place to newness of life. Rituals are needed to carry the baptized over transitions and to place them back on the path to healing.

In times of suffering, healing rituals can be the boat to carry someone who is languishing on his or her own to the other shore of wholeness. In some cases, a person may just need insight and perspective on his or her situation, enabling her or him to act, change, move forward, or start anew. But other times, persons need someone else to take the initiative to act as an adult on their behalf. Frequently, persons realize they are at a loss but cannot imagine vitality and have no faith or hope of living differently. They may seek a new life, but are unable to find it on their own. Thus sometimes people need rescuing by a caring person who can navigate a boat over to them, help them on, and row them to the other side. Rituals of healing are like being ferried across the water.

Healing is a large category. Experiences that call for rites of healing include giving birth to a stillborn child, being abused by a relative or another trusted person, death anniversaries, losing a job, family estrangement, undeserved ostracism or public ridicule, slander, bullying, torture, or any physical or spiritual discomfort that keeps people from being whole and fully alive.

Healing, which was Jesus' work, is the work of the church. Churches have offered *prayer* (including laying on of hands and/or anointing with oil) for the sick and those in spiritual pain; *exorcism* for those not able to be themselves (with strong and experienced leadership only); and *healing of memories*[16] (among others) for those suffering with fear and resentment. Churches have offered *confession*—penance, reconciliation, absolution—for those in spiritual dis-ease, including people who are ill, who feel impure or tainted, or who feel guilty and need to forgive or receive forgiveness. Churches have offered rites for physical healing, for example, as a person enters into a long process of treatment for a chronic or tenacious disease, and rites of thanksgiving following cure. Rites around the end of life also fall into the healing category, as do anniversary rituals.

Such situations may signal to a sensitive, caring, pastoral person that spiritual ritual intervention may be helpful. When people have done all they can do and they have reached the end of the road, hopelessness can set in. Since a person is rarely able to engender one's own wholeness, it is especially valuable to have a ritually competent, compassionate mediator with the vision to see what is needed and to offer the care of the church. A healing liturgy can be a gift, an act of grace (*charis*): someone(s) to share the burden, awaken their faith, and enable them to express their hope and trust in God through action: through ritual action.

And it is not just in times of pain and suffering that persons may need effective ritual. In times of transition, a life-passage ritual can be a stile over the fence to greener pasture. Indeed, "building stiles over the fences of life" is an apt metaphor for both the normalcy and the difficulty of passing from one terrain of life to another. The normal human life, helpfully compared to a journey, leads us through rocky paths, open trails, steep climbs. We make our way with singing or lamenting, alone or together, smoothly or laboriously. But sometimes, we come to a fence, a wall, a barrier that we cannot pass through on our own. This is a critical moment. Sometimes we just stay put, setting up camp by the fence, creating little villages—even deciding that this was where we were going all along. Sometimes we exhaust ourselves, railing at our fate, hands curled around what seem our prison bars. Sometimes we wait. Sometimes we struggle, climbing and falling, bandaging our wounds and struggling again. Reflecting on the waiting or the struggling may shift our perspective, even prepare us for the next stage of the journey. Friends or strangers may wait or struggle with us, perhaps suggesting techniques for vaulting or sources of poles. But sometimes, to get over the barrier, we need a climbing structure. We need a stile. We need a ritual.

Life-passage rites, then, can serve as support ladders over potentially difficult obstacles in life. Christians are familiar with baptism, house blessing, or confessing a spiritual burden to a trusted other. But there are other critical occasions when the church has typically not been involved. For example, being adopted into a new family is a major life shift, for which the legal paperwork does not express the tremendous loss and gain for both the child and the family. Retirement is a huge ending, yet without a rite that also shows it to be a beginning, persons can feel empty or useless, and can even die within the first year. But how would someone conduct a retirement rite? Where would we begin to think about an adoption rite? Just having some basic principles as guidelines could enable someone with ritual sensitivity, theological understanding, and empathic compassion to reach out to a vulnerable person, to offer a caring liturgy.

Some rites serve both purposes: healing and passage. Sometimes a passage cannot occur without attention to the pain that makes the person fearful of climbing the stile. Examples of such situations include finding a birth place, divorce, release from prison, returning from war and trying to fit in again to an utterly different world while making peace with memories and injuries. My goal is to enable leaders to recognize persons facing such dead-ends who, without a rite to help them over the fence, may stop, their growth stunted.

3. *The role of the churches is to learn, teach, and practice the conducting of such rites.* When I first started working on this topic in the 1980s, I noticed that the first books out about ritualization were not Christian. For some Christians, the word *ritual* connotes "impersonal" or "inauthentic" or even "pagan." Once I had a student who always thought of ritual as empty. Baffled after my lecture, he puzzled, "What you said made it seem as if there could be *good* ritual."

His perspective startled me. He had learned something, and so had I. There is indeed empty ritual, dead ritual, pro forma ritual. Grimes has a whole chapter in his book *Ritual Criticism* on ritual failure,[17] and since then, I've found additions to his taxonomy. Worse than the meaningless events my student rightly feared, rituals can also actively be death dealing. One thinks of satanic rituals, ritual killings from the Roman arenas to the French Revolution to current ritual beheadings by terrorists. Less obvious are rituals that name half-truths and are thus dishonest, careless, or ignorant: ritual leadership that attends to the family mourners, for example, but leaves no space for other grievers' loss, rituals where symbols are misused, rituals that inadvertently proclaim the culture but not the gospel. Ritual is powerful and works beneath the level of consciousness, as Bell has shown. Its strength is that people can enter fully into the event and let their "observer" mind rest. But this strength can be distorted, and people can be manipulated. There is a necessary ethic attached to any leading of worship.

It is the role of the churches to apply ritual ethics to the conducting of weekly worship. Ritual is a human phenomenon of which Christian worship is a part. The churches have a stake in learning to do rites to help the baptized grow and mature. But this is based on a prior stake in doing worship well, for regular Sunday worship is the sustaining food for every life crisis. And as startling a realization as it would have been to my student, worship *is* ritual. Ritual is a universal human phenomenon carried out in such specific ways that persons may not be aware that when they attend Sunday worship they are engaged in ritual. But they are. And not just any ritual; they are engaged in the specific kind of ritual called Christian worship—the wondrous Sunday gathering that makes palpable Christians' identity as the ones covenanted to Christ who gather week by week on the day of his resurrection.

Because the churches' primary converse week after week is worship, the churches in fact have implicit ritual knowledge,[18] which aside from the content of worship (preaching, praying, singing), is itself a gift the churches could make to the world. Christians live week by week in relationship to their worship, which is celebrated in relationship to their lives. Christians have a liturgical way of life that is its own kind of expertise, of which most Christians and many pastors are unconscious. Many have never thought about the ongoing relationship of worship to life as a kind of expertise, a knowledge, a practice that can be a gift to others. It is the churches' specific role to engage this knowledge to create caring liturgies for its members.

4. *The church has a tradition of creating rites as part of a process of conversion in faith and growth in Christ.* The early church provided a model for enabling spiritual and behavioral conversion and Christian maturing through a series of rites in preparing persons for baptism. Called the catechumenate, this three- to five-year process[19] was an effective rhythm of learning punctuated by rituals. In the first three centuries, this catechumenal rhythm engaged would-be Christians in a pattern and path of spiritual growth in community, ethics, belief, and understanding, a journey on which progress was marked by means of rites leading up to baptism. These were the rites of initiation.

My primary basis for inviting the churches to bring their ritual knowledge to consciousness in order to engage it responsibly for the good of their people lies in this early church ritual practice related to the making of new Christians. While I cannot detail the process here, what is most important is that the early church understood its role to be enabling seekers to grow in such a way that they were utterly changed more and more into the likeness of Christ. Their progress on this path was punctuated by rites: admission to the order of catechumens, enrollment, and baptism. The first two rites, though not considered sacraments per se, were holy, pastoral, and functional. The rites connected the individuals' journeys to the community's journey. They were conducted as the person was ready to be carried to the next phase.

There is no reason not to continue this pattern after baptism. Creating liturgies to mark healing and transition on the Christian conversionary journey is a foundational practice that should now also be appropriated for postbaptismal catechesis, for the journey leading all the way to Christians' second baptism at death. The "awe-inspiring"[20] rites of our conversion should not end, but begin again, at baptism. It is the role of the churches to cultivate, teach, and practice rites of transition and healing for the postbaptismal progress of every Christian into maturity in Christ.

5. *Christian ritual makers are responsible to cultivate competence in order to create holy rituals that are liberating and life giving.* Like the rites of initiation, all of which are part of the initiation process culminating in baptism, rites after baptism are part of the baptismal process of life in Christ by the Spirit until this life is complete. Again, all churches are familiar with the ritual care that happens (or not) at weddings and funerals and the difficulties posed in offering such care. In addition to weddings and funerals, Roman and Anglican churches are familiar with the seven rites that twelfth-century Scholastic bishop Peter Lombard identified as sacraments, of which four are rites of passage (baptism, confirmation, marriage, ordination), two are healing rites (anointing the sick, confession), and the seventh, of course, is Holy Communion. So natural and familiar are these rites that caring church folk may engage in prayer with laying on of hands without thinking of it as a ritual action or making it a ritual event. Beyond the familiar rites, however, are other rituals and symbolic actions that give life and freedom. For example, when someone places a cross, flowers, and a teddy bear by the side of the road where a fatal accident occurred, the truth of the person's lament is ritualized, contributing to the grief process toward restored inner freedom and life.

Unfortunately, however, sometimes it is easier to recognize competently led, life-giving ritual in contrast with ritual that is not. Rites that go bad are what Grimes calls "ritual infelicity."[21] Rites with unbalanced symbolic rupture (with inadequate strategic contrast), or that are out of context (not situational), or draw attention to themselves (are so self-conscious that effectiveness leaks away), or are death dealing (mediating power that is nonredemptive) because they ignore the focal person or misuse symbol or otherwise fall short of honoring all the participants or bearing the focal person across the stile or the lake—at least all these rites are failed ritual.

Death-dealing rituals, like those of social scapegoating and bully-ing, or ritual suicides in cults such as Jonestown in Guyana in 1978 or Heaven's Gate in San Diego in 1997, are rituals on the extreme end of the spectrum. However, there are many ways to fail in ritual action that are not all the way over on the death end. Like so many human shortfalls that come from simply not seeing—inner blindness—many ritual shortfalls are inadvertent, even done with good intention. When the results are not good, however, sometimes the ritual maker never finds out.

In an ecclesial example, one pastor decided to change the pattern of invitation for communion one Sunday, hoping to add meaning to the rite, and invited persons to come up as family groups to receive together. As it happened, however, a long-time member of the congregation who had recently been widowed and was in the thick of grief had finally managed to attend worship that Sunday after an extended absence. When it was her turn, the horror hit her: she'd have to walk up all alone, a public dem-onstration of the loss of her husband. She just couldn't face it; it was too soon. So she stayed in her seat. The thing she needed most—communion, with God and her brothers and sisters in her faith family, when she was facing lack of communion at her dining table—was suddenly made con-tingent on having a nuclear family with whom to receive. It was months before she came back to worship. The pastor never knew.

The pastor's intent was good: the desire to make a link between the intimacy of family and intimacy with God. However, it was not thought through theologically. Paul's theology of adoption points to a new com-munity, the body of Christ, a family that puts us with people we wouldn't normally choose, the ones "called out" (*ec + clesia*) into ministry, the "beloved community," as Martin Luther King Jr. most famously called it. We are each adopted into this family by baptism. God has thus given us a family, so that we are never bereft, whether single, or far away, or expe-riencing loss and grief. God is closer to us than our breath, but has also given us a flesh-and-blood family in the church. Pastorally, this woman very much needed to be reminded of and embraced by her new family in Christ at the time when her husband, her primary human source of intimacy, had died. And if she couldn't turn to her church family, where could she go? Without ritual ethics and competence, ritual can fail to be true, and can fail to give life.

But there is another ritual failure that is also a concern: *rituals that are needed but never conducted.* These are the ones that the churches could do, but don't. While there is risk in developing occasional rituals for persons suffering or in transition, there is also risk in not doing so. This book is filled with principles and stories so as to increase skill and confidence in generating spiritual pastoral liturgies to carry the baptized along their life journeys into the mystery of full humanity and divinity in Christ. Readers will reduce the risk of this last error: "no ritual when needed," or "ritual absence."

The conducting of life-giving worship, and indeed, of any kind of ritual action, requires *ritual competence*[22] to know when and how to ask for, plan, lead, or support rituals that mediate healing, transition, and life. I encourage you to practice ritual resourcefulness, but only with ritual competence. And practice this ritual competence with a ritual ethic, bringing to bear your own maturity and morality and the best practices of ministry,[23] always beginning with prayer and engaging the intention to follow the Spirit in serving truth, freedom, the common good, and the best interest of all the participants toward healing and redemption.

This book, then, argues that *rituals are desperately needed to enable human growing and maturing, both through times of suffering and through times of transition*—not just at the four life-cycle stages biologists have identified,[24] but at numerous other moments as well. *It is the role of the churches, which have a stake in the maturing of every baptized Christian, to learn, teach, and practice the conducting of such rites with life-giving competence.*

What follows are six chapters to enable pastors and others to evoke the mystery of God's care through holy ritual for the sake of healing and transition for members of the body of Christ. "Creative Rites" explains *what* we seek, and "Ritual Midwives" describes *who.* "Metaphors and Symbols," "Ritual Honesty," and "Holy Sacrifice" are *how.* "The Paschal Mystery" is *why* those with ritual fluency and spiritual competence would offer caring liturgies. These principles are offered for rituals on behalf of those persons who specifically live the Christian story, for rituals are attached to a story and an ethic.[25] Readers from other traditions would have to test and develop caring ritual principles for persons who live a different story and ethic.

It is my hope that the six principles, explained and illustrated with stories, will help Christians discern whether and what kind of worshipful ritual action may be of loving spiritual assistance to another. May these principles help pastors shape the processes by which personal ecclesial ritual can be created to give life, enable growth, and strengthen ministry.

1

Creative Rites

Assessing Pastoral Ritual Need

🕊 We begin by taking up the challenge of perceived conflict between the great story of creation and redemption and the person's story, and presenting creative rituals as the way to make a deeper and effective connection between those stories. There are two kinds of effectiveness. First is the *theological/doctrinal*, which is how the great story has been interpreted institutionally. Next is *experiential/operational* effectiveness, which is how persons have or have not been able to deepen in faith through ritualizing their stories. Both kinds of effectiveness can be honored through competently creating rituals that are spiritual and ethical. The starting point for doing so is care for persons whose stories render them spiritually vulnerable.

In their engaging book *Mighty Stories, Dangerous Rituals,* a teacher of pastoral care, Herbert Anderson, and a teacher of liturgy, Ed Foley, make the point that stories and rituals go together.[1] Sometimes there are rituals without stories (thin or empty rites), but other times there are stories without rituals (ritual absence). For stories to be celebrated and made real, they need rituals. But not just any ritual; they need the right rite, an ethical rite, the spiritually appropriate rite. They need a rite that interprets their story in light of the great story.

Indeed, creative pastors across the generations have understood it to be their spiritual pastoral role to bring the liturgical worshipful resources of the churches to bear upon the needs of their people, from retirement and empty nest to illness and loss of every kind. There have been official and unofficial rites and supplemental services, privately and as part of Sunday morning worship. Done in the Russian Orthodox Church, they are called *moliebens*;[2] in the Roman Catholic Church, *sacramentals*[3] or *blessings*;[4] in the Episcopal Church, *occasional services*[5] or *pastoral offices*;[6] in other Protestant denominations, *rituals of pastoral care*[7] or *liturgy in the gaps*.[8] Since the second half of the twentieth century, such rites have been done by women for women in what has been known as "women-church," feminist liturgy, and the women's liturgical movement.[9] And in the twentieth-century radical renewal, begun in the openness of Vatican Council II (1962–65) and continuing in new worship books in major Western denominations, there has been an awakening to the need for spiritual support of all the baptized toward fullness of their lives and ministries. The church's liturgical wisdom, when turned toward ritual action beyond Sundays, can mediate the ongoing grace of God unleashed at baptism. There is a quiet yet growing sense that rites in the churches are one important means to enable the baptized to grow fully into the likeness of Christ and to carry them over the stiles of "stuckness" into transition and across the pools of pain to healing.[10]

Rites of healing and transition, then, are not a new idea. What's new is the awareness that the rites in official worship books are insufficient. There can never be enough books of rites to cover all the occasions when rituals of healing and transition are needed, both for groups and for individuals. What's new is the awareness that if churches really want to engage the authority of the laity in ministry, they must support their maturation in every way possible, including with ritual. Conversation, therapy, and desire are important means to a person's growth, but sometimes they are inadequate to enable persons to really change; a ritual is necessary to enact the change. What's new is the awareness that creating particular rites for specific circumstances requires a skill set, a gift for ministry, and a call that may or may not be synchronous with ordination. Typically, those educated in rite making and rite leading are the ones assigned to do that work: clergy. However, not all clergy are gifted or called to engender life-giving, healing rites for others, but some laypersons are so called.

It is the role of the churches to learn, teach, and practice the conducting of both corporate and personal rites with life-giving competence. This book is specifically focused on personal rites, offering principles so that called and gifted persons who have the skills and desire will be better able to generate and conduct rites needed to support the fullness of life and ministry of all those baptized into Christ (and others as well).

So here begin six ritual-creating principles intended to help spiritual leaders make rites in relationship to personal stories that need to be acknowledged and honored. My goal is to awaken ritual awareness, invite ritual competence, and build practical theory, which are needed both for carefully planned rites as well as for quickly determined improvised rites. My intention is to awaken a liturgical spirituality with an application in pastoral ritual practice.

But because ritual as a spiritual-pastoral practice is not new, yet has been largely latent, and because the need is so great now as the churches are edging out of Christendom (with its privilege but also its cultural syncretism), it is important to step back and take a fresh look at how good rites are made, and what process is needed to assure that unintended negative consequences do not arise. Some leaders will see the value of intentional "custom-made" rites as a source of spiritual healing and growth, but may not have the ritual competence to carry them off. Others are not inclined to attempt this ritual work, so that people with a spiritual-ritual need find themselves bereft.

This chapter begins the process of addressing both groups by opening the way for composing rites consciously and competently, the way music-theory books open the means for composing beautiful and satisfying music. Books of rites are a bit like musical scores: they are not the music; they do not convey the hoped-for spirit of a rite. This book instead offers transferable principles to guide the making of rites with a fitting "feel" or spirit. Supporting the practice of spiritual care through rites of transition and healing is of crucial importance in the contemporary challenges of the life of the church. The rhythm of principle and story intends to engage the mind and heart of spiritual ritual practice.

One story in particular will unfold chapter by chapter. It is about Joanie, who faced a devastating divorce. Her painful situation involved *both* transition *and* suffering. The primary actors in this ritual situation have given permission for me to recount their story (although their names have been changed). Joanie is the one who requested the rite.

This story is not a "case study," but an illustrative ritual that really happened. It is not an idealized ritual. It is, in fact, different from the ideal in some ways because there was no official presider, there was little time to prepare and some elements one might usually plan (such as an ending) did not occur. However, I have selected this ritual for two reasons. First, although it does not include all of the principles expounded here, it exemplifies many of them very well. Second, it demonstrates real-life circumstances and challenges that any ritual leader may have to face. For example, in my experience, it is not uncommon for someone to realize at the eleventh hour that one is set to participate in a rite for which one does not know what to do, which was the case with Joanie. I have had many last-minute telephone calls seeking ritual coaching (for example, "My father's funeral will be in two days; I have the place, the flowers, the reception planned, and the ritual leader booked—we just don't know what to do"). As in other urgent situations, one must offer one's best in the moment. Further, there are times when persons want to ritualize an occasion and they do not seek the guidance of a professional. They muster what resources they have and "just do it."

Ritual, after all, is a human language, and anyone may attempt to "speak" it and conduct one. Without guidance, however, sometimes a ritual misses an opportunity or falls short or can even be harmful. However, one reason for offering what I have learned about ritual making is so that people will have more resources, readily available and further in advance, in order to be more prepared for such circumstances.

In Joanie's case, my role was as an out-of-town friend who was invited to assist over the telephone with suggestions, questions, care, and prayer. Let's tune in.

Joanie's Story

The telephone rang. It was my friend Joanie calling from across the country. But it turns out she wasn't calling just to chat. She had news—sad news.

"The divorce is finally, really going to happen, Sue. And Frank's coming with the truck next Saturday to take half the furniture."

My mind reeled. Divorce! I knew this had been a difficult marriage for years. I knew how many workshops, therapists, counseling sessions, and prayer vigils Joanie had attended, and I had some idea of the tears she had shed, the strategies she had tried, the struggles she had endured. I did not know Frank's struggles so much, but I knew he had them. Yet each time they'd had a crisis, they somehow had always come through it. But something had happened; a decision had been made. The marriage struggles were ending. Now there would be divorce and a different set of struggles.

My heart longed to support her. But all I could utter was, "Oh, Joanie! Oh, I'm so sorry to hear this news. You've worked so hard and so long for this marriage."

"I'm sorry, too," she replied in a subdued tone. "But after all this, if I'm honest with myself, I have to acknowledge that it really is over. Something else has surfaced, Sue, and what we have now is not a marriage. I've been so afraid to let it go. Who in the world would I be as a single woman? But now, I'm finally beginning to claim the possibility of an identity as myself, apart from all the links and dependencies of marriage."

This was a huge step for Joanie. I was struck at the level of self-knowledge she had gained and her ability, in the midst of the pain and loss and failure of this marriage in which she had invested so much, to see the bigger picture. How emotionally and spiritually mature she had become, and was becoming, in this crucible of relationship and heartache! She had wanted this marriage to work so very, very much. But one person cannot make a marriage.

"He's moving on. He has an apartment already. I guess that's why he wants to take his things, and some of our things. It's sad, and it's really difficult. But there's one good thing here that I want to talk with you about. Remember how I've asked over the years for us to ritualize some of our transitions?"

I knew very well. Joanie and Frank were from a liturgical tradition, so that the language of ritual was one in which they were both fluent. Yet, for whatever reason, Frank had not agreed to ritualize any of the various steps and turns they had taken over the years, nor would he celebrate renewed attempts to stay together in new commitments through many trials.

"This time, he said yes! So next Saturday, before we divide up the house and he takes his belongings, we'll be able to ritualize the end of our household, and—I guess—the end of our marriage."

Even as I realized how emotionally draining it would be to ritualize the death of their fragile and hard-kept marriage, I felt a certain relief that the ritual could take place. In the back of my mind, I had been trying to imagine—to empathize with—what Joanie would feel waking up on Sunday in "their" house with all its memories, only to find it half-empty, pain visible everywhere. A ritualization, however laborious in the near-term, might make it possible to contain the disorientation and to place the pain in a larger life-giving context, giving her new grounding and energy afterward. I wanted to affirm her wisdom in asking for a rite and to reassure her. But all I could think of were truisms about how a ritual would mark the death of this marriage, and that as hard and painful and sad as that would be, it would also be the one way to enable new life—two new lives. Yet this was not a time for pedantic truisms. This was a time for care and empathy.

But then a thought struck me—hadn't she said next week? All the other rites I had done took longer to prepare. I considered how I might suggest taking two or three weeks to get ready for such an important and emotional event. "Did you say he was coming next Saturday? Do you think . . . ?"

"Yes," she interrupted, with energy. "Next Saturday. So I've asked two couples from church who have been very close to the two of us to be with us in this." Ah. So Joanie was fortunate to have a whole week to prepare, and she had already been at work.

"So I've got the time, and I've got the people. I'm just not sure what we're supposed to do. That's why I'm calling you, Sue. What shall we do?"

The Problem of Resistance

When someone is in the hospital, no one needs to be convinced that the church family must visit. In the hospital room, the visitor might hold hands, pray, read Scripture, lay hands on the person in prayer or blessing, sing, listen, or anoint with healing oil. All these actions are signs of the love and care of the sick person's sisters and brothers in the faith. They *do* love. They are actions that express love by bringing God's comforting word, a loving touch, a trusted and receptive presence. These persons, books, hands, oil, and prayers are outward signs of God's love through the church, and are therefore understood as sacramental in the broad sense. While the visitor may be the only person in the room with the hospitalized person, the whole church is there represented in that visitor.

Joanie, however, was not in the hospital. She was hurting, vulnerable, and facing a huge life change. But because she was not part of a recognized healing system, it would not occur to many (perhaps most) in the churches that she, too, needed outward and visible signs of God's loving care and spiritual guidance in her vulnerability. Joanie's ritual, which would be held in her house, would be an appropriate series of actions parallel to what would be offered to someone in the hospital. Some ecclesial rites are not offered in the church house, not offered on Sunday morning, not even offered by the pastor.

Rites can be personal and ecclesial, which means that while they are private and confidential, they are done on behalf of the whole *ecclesia,* the family of faith, the body of Christ. Rites of confession or reconciliation are examples. It isn't the priest or pastor who forgives: it is God who forgives, and the priest or pastor pronounces in faith God's forgiveness on behalf of the whole church. God's spiritual graces often come through the church, by its lay and clerical ministers.

In many cases, a person's need does not involve hospitalization and thus is not so readily recognized. Like Joanie, persons may be in spiritual anguish, but perhaps no one will imagine offering a sacramental ritual response if it is not a common situation. But because of the need for outward and visible signs of God's presence and the community's love, the imagination of church folks must be expanded for them to recognize and assess the spiritual need for a rite. Spiritual growth and healing can happen anywhere, even outside the confessional or hospital room.

It is important that a ritual caregiver have a broad imagination to recognize when a person is vulnerable and would be helped by an ecclesial ritual action, either a rite that already exists or a rite that may never have been done before. To imagine various kinds of ritual need, it may be helpful to review Gilbert Ostdiek's four categories of situations needing ritualization,[11] the first two of which are loosely transitions, and the other two loosely healing moments (although any particular situation may be either or both). First, Ostdiek says ritual may be needed in "moments of significant transition" when "people are wrestling with issues of continuity and change" (42), like Joanie. Second, a rite may be needed in threshold moments when "a significant experience unfolds over a period of time" and the person can be helped by ritualizing the steps or stages (44): a child's first day of school or Ostdiek's example of a soon-to-be-married couple each ritualizing leaving their parents' homes before celebrating the wedding. Beyond such transitions, Ostdiek also names a third situation: when "there is a significant need to express or discern the meaning of our lives," because meaning seems to be disintegrating or because one is moving to embrace a new identity or vocation (43), such as facing a debilitating or long-term illness or when one's almost-grown child feels estranged and leaves home, cutting off contact. And fourth, rituals can help "in situations which call for personal commitment and group support," when risks and possibilities require a "safe place" (44) to face chosen or unchosen change. Ostdiek's categories reveal specific situations of vulnerability involving risk or change when ritualizing could make a life-giving difference. A competent ritual maker who cultivates ritual imagination may be able to hear such a ritual need, and then discern what kind of rite might best respond.

So why aren't healing or transitional rituals offered very often? Sometimes a competent pastor will decide that offering to help create a ritual is not the most appropriate response. For example, while the person's vulnerability and need for ritual action may be recognized, there may not be a skilled ritual maker available to lead planning, without which there may be an appropriate fear of doing a ritual in a way that is more harmful than helpful. Or a skilled ritual maker may recognize that the person's situation calls for lament or celebration, perhaps with family or friends, but is not appropriate for an ecclesial worshipful ritual. Christian ecclesial rites create holy space for ultimate stakes: God's relationship to the community of faith in death and resurrection.

But more often, the option of offering a caring ritual does not arise at all. There are several reasons for this.

- Conducting a ritual might not occur to the pastor because there isn't one listed in one's denominational worship book, so it must not be authorized and therefore shouldn't be done, or the pastor doesn't know what to do.
- Organizing rites that first have to be invented takes lots of time. A busy pastor's mind may avoid an idea that would seem to put her or him on overload.
- In some cases there just may not be enough interest or compassion to expend the energy needed for a ritual. The focal persons are surviving, yet the motivation to see them *thrive* may be lacking.
- Because some situations, like divorce, represent a broken covenant, especially a covenant avowed in church before the Lord, an ecclesial rite might be misconstrued as celebrating or condoning that which falls in the realm of sin.
- Even if the pastor is not concerned about ritualizing sin, such a ritual creates witnesses to failure and brokenness, which is hard to see in others, and can hit too close to home for those who have experienced similar situations.

There are two additional resistances to offering a caring liturgy, which we will discuss here. One is "unrecognized vulnerability." Sometimes, pastors do not empathize with the person's spiritual pain that renders them *unable* to act. Pastors may resist the idea that persons are so vulnerable or have reached such a sticking point that they cannot pass

beyond it without help. But persons can need a rescue. They need someone else to take initiative. When those around them do not recognize the
gravity of the blockage, nor initiate help, empathy is needed to see how
ritual empowerment could help the vulnerable. The second resistance is
the "dilemma reason," to which we now turn.

Resistance as a Dilemma between Theology and Experience

Sometimes rituals are not offered because the pastor can feel caught
between the doctrinal practices of the church on the one hand, and the
empathic desire to care for a hurting parishioner on the other hand. There
is always a tension between the churches' theology of sin, humanity, sacrament, the church, and so forth, and the immediate pastoral need in a
specific situation. Many pastors have been torn, heart from mind, intuition from reason, pastoral instinct from theological norm, wondering, "If
I support a hurting parishioner, will I be compromising moral standards
the church upholds?" The tension in this ambiguity has been so great as
to press pastors to make an infelicitous choice: one or the other. Here is
an example:

*Dennis came to his pastor the week before deployment to a war zone and asked to
be baptized. "I thought you were baptized, Dennis."*

*"Well, I was, Pastor Blaine—but I was a baby back then. Now I'm going to
be in harm's way, and—well, I just want to be sure I know that I belong to Christ
and that he is watching over me. I want to feel the water and hear the words, so
my body will never forget."*

*Blaine was tempted. It's an incarnational religion, after all—in the flesh.
But he knew from seminary that rebaptism is a no-no, and doing so would split
the local clergy group.*

*"Dennis, I hear you. But God's promises are sure, and God never lets go of
his own. Do you really want to make God prove his love? And if you get isolated
later, overseas, what will stop you from asking for baptism again? We just don't
rebaptize."*

Dennis's face was shocked. "But I want to be close to God! And you are my
pastor. *I'm sure the military chaplain would do it—but my family is here. You
wouldn't deny me, would you?"*

Naming the edges of the tension can help map the terrain in between. Anthropologists Sally Moore and Barbara Myerhoff provide a helpful description of the two sides to this dilemma. Theological understanding (of how God works, for example), Moore and Myerhoff call "doctrinal efficacy" (or, *theological effectiveness*): here, the doctrinal claims of God's power and effectiveness in worship and Christian ritual that are affirmed in Scripture, tradition, and reason. In contrast, the actual subjective ritual experience of persons, they call "operational efficacy." Such empirical results or experienced changes in persons that occur through or resulting from Christian rituals will be called here *experienced effectiveness*, referring to what the person experiences from worship or ritual.[12]

Assessing the soldier and his pastor's dilemma by affirming both understands that each is imagining a different but equally important effect that would come from a rite. Dennis is seeking *experienced effectiveness*. The pastor wants this for Dennis; but he also recognizes the power and need for *theological effectiveness* by virtue of the church's understanding of how God works. Dennis is not trying to challenge this belief, for he affirms the church's meaning. Rather, without having a word for it, Dennis is crying out for effectiveness he can feel—experience—inside himself. Myerhoff writes:

> What Moore calls the *doctrinal efficacy* [*theological effectiveness*] of religious ritual is provided by the explanations a religion itself gives of how and why ritual works. The explanation is within the religious system and is part of its internal logic. The religion postulates by what causal means a ritual, if properly performed, should bring about the desired results. A religious ritual refers to the unseen cosmic order, works through it and operates on it directly through the performance. . . . Doctrinal efficacy is a matter of postulation. As the intrinsic explanation, it need merely be affirmed.[13]

The theological effectiveness of baptism, for example, has been articulated in *Baptism, Eucharist and Ministry*, the ecumenical statement on baptism affirmed, with tremendous effort, by some three hundred Christian churches worldwide.[14] Dennis's pastor knows this, and knows the depth of meaning held in common: God is the actor in baptism, the giver of the gift.[15] By water and the Holy Spirit, in the name of the Trinity, and by the intentional work of the church through its designated pastors, the one baptized is washed new, freed from sin and united to Christ in his death and resurrection.[16] Baptism is irrevocable. God's powerful, loving action makes the baptizand part of Christ's body, forever. The initiate freely responds to God by receiving baptism.

Baptism is effective. Whether or not the newly baptized person feels different does not change the fact of our belief in God's power through the sacrament (or ordinance): the person *is* now different, bonded with Christ in his death and resurrection. This firm faith is *theological effectiveness.*

The effectiveness of theology is not the same as the effectiveness of experience, however, as Dennis wants his pastor to see. Not everyone remembers her or his baptism. Not everyone is old enough to have felt the water, to have labored and prepared so as to leave their fears and resentments in the depths, to have come out to the joyous song of the congregation's Alleluia! Not everyone has an embodied memory as a reference point to recall, in the bad times, that they in fact belong to God. While baptism is true and powerful whether or not one is conscious of it, still, without the embodied memory as reference, it can be harder to pull up the power of one's baptism in times of need. And sometimes, this lack of memory is a source of pain. In contrast, then, according to Moore,

> outcome or consequence . . . is attributed to *operational efficacy* [*experienced effectiveness*]. Results, successes, failures, are part of the operational effects of a ritual. These are the empirical questions in analysis. For example, healing ceremonies may or may not make a patient feel better. Political ceremonies may or may not succeed in rearranging images, may succeed or fail in attaching positive or negative balances to certain ideas or persons. Rites may vary greatly in successfully convincing their participants and communicating their messages. Such questions about communicative, social/ psychological effects are [experienced, or] operational.[17]

Experienced effectiveness, then, has to do less with what rituals say than with what they do. In contrast with the official theological meaning, operational effectiveness has to do with the *experience of the worshiper,*[18] with the *meaning experienced.*

Experienced and theological meanings and effects are not necessarily mutually exclusive, but they also don't necessarily occur at the same time. If Dennis had been baptized as an adult with all the conversionary preparation, his embodied experience with all its memories would have happened at the time of his baptism. Having been baptized as an infant, however, the sacrament's theological effectiveness took hold, and no doubt the Spirit's work continues to operate in his life. But his own embodied memory from such a young age is not available to him.

What's the answer to this dilemma? Pastor Blaine felt constrained to choose between theological truth and experienced truth, between the church's fount of understanding and Dennis's pastoral need. In this case, Blaine succumbed to choosing and opted to rebaptize him. The pastor chose to mediate a rite for Dennis's experience at the expense of theological effectiveness, the faith of the church. Therefore, he solved one real problem by creating another one.

Yet the dilemma would be solved if the pastor spoke the language of ritual with sufficient imaginative fluency to offer Dennis an embodied experience of God's presence and love, on Sunday with his faith family, without re-baptizing him. The third way, a creative liturgy, allows recognition of ritual need, the holding of theological integrity, and the creativity to assess and embrace the most fitting solution: a Christian ritual.

What the pastor did not realize is that there is a step between hearing the request and responding. This in-between step is *assessing the appropriate ritual* that could offer the best ritual care in this particular situation: for ritual, as Bell points out, is specific to the person and the situation. This requires understanding what a ritual would need to effect, how it fits or doesn't fit within denominational theologies of worship and order, and who would need to be involved to assure that a rite doesn't open floodgates no one present is able to manage. Any assessment of what kind of ritual is needed must consider both the focal person's heart-cry for stability and support for a changed reality, and the church's theological understanding of what rituals and sacramental rites do, what they're for. Competent assessment of ritual need considers a ritual's effectiveness both experientially, in the worshiper's need and experience, and theologically, in the denomination's belief and offering of what a ritual means.

In this case, both the pastor and Dennis are "right." Baptism is not repeatable. The pastor is right to assert this. Yet Dennis is also right that his life has come to a terrible transition, a time of danger, where an acknowledgment of and recommitment to his relationship with God is clearly called for. So how does one handle two "rights" that seem mutually exclusive?

Some would say, "This is a clear conflict between theological and pastoral needs—and since the pastoral always trumps the theological, the pastor should do it anyway." Others would say, "This is a clear conflict between the theological, which is what the whole church believes, and the pastoral, which is the need of one person. You can't have every individual undoing what the church spends tremendous energy trying to work out. Dennis should give it up."

However, there is a third way of assessing this situation that does not pit good theology against good pastoring—because, in truth, *both* are important and *both* must be upheld. The pastor's very tension may press him to choose one or the other; but in the economy of God's abundance, "choosing between" is not necessary in this situation. It is possible, ritually, to solve the dilemma and honor both perspectives through the third way of *offering a creative ritual*.

Theological efficacy is essential. It counts. For Dennis to leave for battle with the idea, however small, lurking around the edges of his mind, that the effectiveness of God's action, love, and power is only effective *if he feels it* is a pastorally dangerous risk. God is faithful. Once baptized, one's state has changed: one *is* a child of God, one *belongs* to Christ, and nothing in heaven or on earth can change that powerful and liberating reality. Experiential efficacy counts, as well. Christianity is incarnational: God came to earth in the flesh as human, in Christ Jesus. Through the incarnation, all flesh is redeemed; the body is the means by which salvation occurs; the "flesh is the hinge of salvation," as Tertullian puts it. The soldier needed an embodied experience of God's love for him and claim on his life; and, feeling vulnerable, he had come to the church with a pastoral ritual need. The pastor was obligated to meet him in this need the best way possible: with powerful enough symbols to create an embodied memory that could sustain the soldier through impending death-dealing times.

In this case, there already exists a rite that would beautifully offer Dennis what he needed within the existing repertoire of most denominations: a Renewal of Baptismal Vows specifically oriented toward Dennis's new self-giving in military service. In this case, baptismal renewal, which is a rite in books of prayer and worship, could have been adapted and offered as a powerful renewal experience for Dennis with God in Christ by the Spirit, before going off to war.

But sometimes, a pastor chooses the third way without an available rite. Consider Deborah's process in an equally poignant dilemma:

Over the years, Pastor Deborah's congregation had made a point of reaching out to homeless people in their community. The parish was gratified that many homeless neighbors came to worship and participated in the church's outreach ministries, finding a warm welcome and a caring community. One day a homeless couple came to the pastor's office. With bright smiles on their faces, they exclaimed, "Pastor, we want to get married!"

Deborah's heart sank. She knew this man and this woman, and she loved them both. She knew that they were survivors, as well as a source of comfort and support for each other, which was more than some of the others had in similar circumstances. She also knew about their drug addictions, their mixture of truth telling and dissembling, and their emotional immaturity. She knew about their instances of infidelity, especially during times of separation due to incarceration—not to mention their lack of problem-solving skills. All of this caused Deborah great concern.

Given the intention of Christian marriage to be a mature commitment to help each other deepen spiritually through Christ in the Holy Spirit, and the expectation of faithfulness "til death us do part," Deborah recognized that neither of them was in a position to enter into such a vow. Consequently, Deborah found herself in a conflict between her desire, on the one hand, to be experientially effective by responding to their desire to be drawn deeper into the church family, giving them a sign of the church's love that they could experience together and a day they would always remember; and her desire, on the other hand, to be theologically effective by upholding the church's understanding of Christian marriage.

She also wanted to avoid "setting the couple up" for failure and more emotional trauma. She suspected that the psychological tests the church used for premarital counseling sessions would reveal that they were incompatible with each other, and she did not think they were emotionally stable or mature enough to hear or understand and to accept this information, let alone grow from it as intended by the church in using the test. At the same time, Deborah was compelled to be an ethical role model for her congregation, upholding the faithfulness, mutual support, and self-giving love that she preached about for every married and engaged couple in the church. Integrity in Deborah's words and actions was essential for upholding with her people the beliefs they together espoused, and to continue in the role as a trusted pastor and moral leader among them.

Things came to a head one day when the would-be bride came glowing into her office and joyously announced, "I know what I'm going to wear on my wedding day!" At that moment, it became very clear to Deborah that this woman wanted what every bride wants: the chance to be "queen for a day," to have a memory of joy and specialness that no one could ever take away. She yearned for the soul-filling chance to be beautiful, honored, and feted in her church, filled with love and *surrounded by love, standing before the altar to be married to her beloved. Being a bride is an archetypal, universal, and utterly human spiritual longing; and this impoverished homeless woman wanted and expected nothing less.*

The tension was terrible for Deborah, and it only got worse when she spoke to her colleagues about the situation. "Wouldn't you rather see them get married in the church, where they can not only experience the grace of God but also the love of their church family?" they prodded. She had managed to refrain from retorting, "Don't you think they've already experienced the grace of God and the love of their church family? Otherwise, they would have drifted away a long time ago, instead of coming confidently to me seeking to be married in our midst."

Having a grand homeless wedding might actually get her photograph in the denominational newspaper! It would be fun for the congregation; and since Deborah was a people pleaser, it would certainly please her to help this couple experience the happiness of their dream fulfilled. However, she also wanted to honor the integrity of Christian marriage as she and her church and the rest of the congregation believed it to be. Would it be cheating or would it be wise to suggest they go to the justice of the peace for a civil ceremony and then have a party for them at the church afterwards?

What is the pastoral as well as the ethical thing to do in this situation? Deborah could lose her orders (or license) if she conducted such a wedding in the name of her denomination (not to mention the state) when she believed it would not last and when she felt it would be more of a burden than a help to the couple. To witness before God vows that she was convinced they could not keep would be an ethical violation, a kind of blasphemy. Besides, if she did marry them—or even encourage them to be civilly married—and their marriage ended up falling apart, how pastoral would that feel to them? Deborah began to notice an acute pain in her neck, and she began to lose sleep over the decision she had to make.

Deborah might have found some freedom if she had had the terms to describe her dilemma between experienced and theological effectiveness. As it was, without names for her tension, she felt torn between her desire to fulfill the couple's expressed request, and her desire to honor the ordinances of the church of which she had been made steward at her ordination. Doing what they asked, or doing nothing—neither approach seemed the right way. In the end, her ritual assessment was that marriage was not the most fitting ecclesial rite for this couple. Yet she did want to offer the care of the community for them.

Ritual Creativity: Solving Dilemmas through the Third Way

What would it take, then, to move to the third way through ritual creativity? The first step is assessing the person's underlying spiritual need beneath their request, in this case, for marriage. The answer is not simple nor can it be shallow. The answer cannot be to do a "pretend wedding." The answer requires truth telling, honesty, ritual competence, and creativity. In assessing spiritual ritual need, it is important not to be limited by what people ask for nor by what the pastor immediately imagines. Assessing spiritual ritual need requires prayer and being open to the Spirit. It requires deep listening.

What is their real heart hunger? This couple may not want a lot of responsibility. Perhaps knowing that their lifestyle is marginal, they long for a way to know they are part of the human community, embraced by their church family. Perhaps they yearn for an outward and visible sign of God's lovingkindness toward them. It could be that they want "normal" lives, and a wedding would be a sign for them of normalcy.

Or maybe they are enduring a particularly heavy time, and they really desire the lightness of celebration, of gifts, of a day to remember, of a photo album to hold as witness that they have a family who loves them and a meaning that embraces them. Or perhaps they want a greater stake in the family of faith. Maybe they are drawn by the desire to know they belong. Perhaps they want to belong to each other in a very real way, and to receive God's blessing. Maybe they want help and support for their lives with each other. It could be that they would like other church members to come to where *they* hang out, beyond the church house.

If Deborah offers discerning questions, and listens out of the silence informed by the Spirit, she may be able to find what loving rite will fill their soul. Such listening is a gift because sometimes the deep tectonic movements in our own souls are hidden from us. Not only that, but God has already been working in the couple's midst. What are the signs of the Lord's presence already at work in their lives? How might they respond to the gifts God has already placed within and before them? How does their desire work within the mission of the people of God to love and serve? What is a next step in their spiritual growth in Christ? Are there those who would sponsor or mentor them or serve as spiritual guides?

As acknowledged earlier, creative rituals are part of the baptismal process of growth toward spiritual maturity. Deborah may consider what would lead to spiritual fulfillment for each person, and then imagine a rite that would express and engender that fulfillment (the first principle). This will be accomplished by following five additional principles: (1) form a planning committee; (2) identify a defining metaphor; (3) plan the rite with ritual honesty (pain and grace, lament and hope); (4) engage the couple in whatever process, even if laborious, would help their passage or healing, so that the rite will manifest giving and receiving, offering and sacrifice; and (5) make the connection between the person's life and Christ's death and resurrection. When the nature of the rite is known, anticipating its celebration can create strong motivation for the formative growth process.

While listening to this couple share their hearts, Deborah would have her theologies ready in mind. God is a God of blessing, of abundance and thanksgiving, of covenant. God calls us to be in covenantal relationship with each other and expects ethical, self-giving care for neighbors and strangers. God is incarnational. God is beauty, truth, and goodness. God calls us to use our gifts for others, such that we ourselves will find joy and fulfillment. God is one and calls us to unity. And God is a God of radical particularity. God cares about these persons' stories and their celebration in the church family.

This heart-listening for their experiential longing stands beside theological effectiveness. Beyond the scope of this chapter, but certainly in the background, is the theological context of Deborah's dilemma, intensified by another set of concerns the churches face around the rite of marriage. Longings for covenant in monogamous union that vary from marriage rites abound. The desire of same-sex couples to receive both civil and ecclesial privileges and blessings is similar. So is the request of elderly couples who are widowed and have found each other as companions in later years, but do not want confusion in their respective children's inheritance. Early in the Eastern church, nonmarried persons sought similar blessing as well as social and legal recognition for alternative households through a rite called *adelphopoiesis* ("making brothers").[19] Deborah's challenge is the challenge of the church: the particularity of ritual need stretches ecclesial systems, yet theological continuity is needed. Creative ritualizing, then, is not only a gift to the couple; it is a gift to the churches.

Ethically, if the pastor is not in a position to do this process or is not ready to offer either marriage or something else, then the pastor is obligated to refer the couple to a pastor and/or a denomination who can help them. Integrating theological and experienced effectiveness may mean holding the line on any given rite, but it also means finding a way to care for the focal persons' real longing when it is of ultimate concern, even if you cannot ritually care for them yourself.

Creative rituals provide a middle way between theological infelicity and pastoral denial. They eliminate the dilemma between existing rite (if any) and no rite. Creative rites enable the baptized to experience the love of the family of faith and growth in the Spirit. Dominance or ignorance of "church rules" will not accomplish this experience. One needs to honor theology while starting with compassionate sensitivity for a person's ritual need arising out of their vulnerability. Indeed, to offer creative rites requires heart-seeking recognition of the other's soul wound.

Resistance as Unrecognized Vulnerability and the Need for Empathy

Besides solving dilemmas, creative rites can also be the solution when persons are living in vulnerabilities unrecognized by themselves and others. Most people don't know to ask for a rite when they need one. Others may ask for a rite without knowing why, like Joanie.

It is perhaps rare that someone in Joanie's situation would be wise enough to realize how important, helpful, and healing it would be to ritualize the dividing of household belongings and the ending of a marriage. Most of us probably wouldn't be able to recognize our need for a rite. I have found it more common for persons to recognize someone else's need for a rite, than to recognize one's own. Endings and beginnings are vulnerable times, memorable times. Look at the drama surrounding the beginning of a marriage—and fittingly so, since a new family is created; their relationships change with their friends, neighbors, and strangers; new responsibilities are claimed; there may be children to raise. But what about the ending of a marriage? Here a family is uprooted; identities are confused; social patterns are gone to seed. This marriage is ending. Ritually marking that end would help friends and neighbors adjust to the changes, would help the husband and the wife accept the wrenching upheaval, and would help the children, extended family, and church family realize and cope themselves while supporting and sustaining the divorcing couple. Ending is needed: lament, and also hope; cross, and also resurrection. God is always at work, blessing and redeeming.

The process of planning a Christian ritual begins with one who has the eyes to see that a ritual is needed. If the vulnerable person's spirit, and/or the person's growth and ministry, could be helped by ritual action, then it is important to look not only for existing rites, but also for a creative third way that holds the person's need for experienced effectiveness in unity with the church's hard-won theological effectiveness. Even prior to the deep listening that will lead to an assessment of whether and what kind of caring ritual may be called for, therefore, the pastoral listener needs to be tuned in to—to be able to empathize with—the spiritual place of vulnerability of the other. It is out of empathic caring that one knows to pay attention to what kind of care would be helpful. There are all kinds of needs persons may have, including healing rituals.

Spiritual Empathy

The primary skill for recognizing and assessing pastoral ritual need is spiritual empathy: compassion and intuitive empathy for the focal person, engaged in dialogue with knowledgeable others.[20] In situations where there is not already a standard rite available, the starting point for competent ritual assessment and creative rite making is compassion, empathy, and deep listening for vulnerability in the feelings and state of the focal person. Ritual assessment is a spiritual practice with a pastoral practical application.

Prayerful discernment in conversation with a trustworthy other can enable a response if someone asks for a ritual, and can also enable a ritual offering if someone cannot recognize a ritual need or know to ask. Spiritual compassion for the affective vulnerability of the focal person from his or her own perspective is a crucial starting point for creative ritual.

This does not deny the importance of other types of starting points. A planning community for a ritual would need people who can attend to the *physical starting point* ("Where are we going to hold this ritual? The church isn't available, and rain is predicted"), *clarity of intent or purpose* ("She and the people important to her need to know how their relationships will be sustained through the move; and it's important that she get a jump-start in building new friendships and a new sense of purpose or work or ministry in the new place"), and *practical* "how to do it" details ("I can't find a ritual for moving out of town in any of my resource books"). As necessary and important as these other starting points are, however, they are not the whole story, and they are not the centerpiece of the rite. A healing ritual that will tend to a person's inner affective spiritual state requires someone who can and will tune in empathically to hear the seemingly conflicting thoughts and feelings operating at once from that person's perspective of his or her own experience.

Empathy takes time. Listening deeply takes energy. Crafting a rite that weaves all the threads into a beautiful whole is an art form that takes focus. Rites can really heal—but rite makers are called upon to give themselves to the process. This is a different process than planning Sunday worship. While liturgy requires theological and symbolic knowledge, and pastoral and practical sensitivity, weekly worship would be unsustainable if pastors had to give the kind of energy Deborah gave to the couple every single week. Spiritual empathy is needed for every liturgy, but it is not the starting point for planning congregational worship.

Pastors can do good worship every week because the typical starting place for regular worship on the Lord's Day is a standard pattern. In liturgical traditions, this is called the *ordo*—the order of worship authorized along with the readings appointed. The liturgical planner then plans the variables: music, sermon, prayers, and circumstances in the world or parishioners' lives. In less liturgical or nonliturgical traditions, one may still start with the usual order of worship even if not officially authorized. Many of my students pull up the congregation's standard worship template on their computer and begin the process of changing readings, call to worship, music, and developing a unifying focus for the Lord's Day services. This usually leads to good worship. It's a practical beginning, and it is sustainable, every week. This is the lifeblood of the people of God, the inhale of their life breath.[21] The pattern is its strength; pastor and people can relax, knowing what's coming.

Starting with the pattern doesn't mean leaders aren't thinking about or caring for their people. Of course they are. Even so, cultivating spiritual empathy could add depth to a worship leader's presiding style and could enable personal celebrations in the Sunday assembly. For example, nearly all the occasional rites that are celebrated by congregations are centered on persons especially lifted before God and embraced in worship. Historically, of the seven sacraments asserted by Peter Lombard and continuing in the Roman Catholic Church,[22] six have focal persons who are the center of the rite and on whose behalf it is enacted: baptism, private confession (the penitent), confirmation, marriage (bride and groom), anointing the sick, and ordination. Plateau rites of initiation in the early church's catechumenal process had catechumens and candidates as focal persons. Congregations today know how to have a "John Thomas Sunday" or to honor mothers or to send the teens away on a mission trip or to celebrate the Boy Scouts. Weddings, funerals, and house blessings are also personal ecclesial rites.

So even when standard rites exist, this spiritual empathic skill of taking the focal person's affective perspective in all its vulnerability is crucial in adapting given rites to particular circumstances. As Bell demonstrates, rituals are situational and strategic, needing particular strategies to help this person through this life crisis. Without such empathy fed by prayer, the spiritual mark can easily be missed.

And then, when there is no standard rite to start with, practical or physical tasks can overlook the core concern: the spirit that needs to be embodied in a rite. *The first principle for transitional or healing ritual[23] in the baptismal process, especially when there is no rite in the book, is to start with the person.* The person is one who belongs to the Creator, who is baptized into Christ, who is a sibling in the Spirit, and is the one for whom you have promised to care. The starting point for rituals in the baptismal process is care for the affective, spiritually vulnerable experience of the focal person on behalf of whom the ritualization will be designed. The healing or transition needed by the focal persons, so that they can continue ever more fully in baptismal living, is both the purpose for and the spirit of the rite to which the ritual leader gives her- or himself.

One of the benefits to the churches of supporting persons to cultivate ritual fluency and competence is that the focal persons, as well as ritual planners and witnesses, take on a deeper sense of connection between the ecclesial community and holy Christian living. When liturgies are focused around particular persons and their situations, the persons themselves can become windows into God's intentions, icons of Christ's grace, epiphanies of the Spirit's love and operation. God was incarnate in a particular human being, and Christ's work was with particular human beings: that rabbi's daughter, this tax collector in the tree, that centurion. Rituals for specific occasions in individual persons' lives are a means of grace received through the churches' worship at the regular weekly service and beyond.

Ethical Limitations in Spiritual Empathy

There are at least three caveats to hold in mind in being guided by empathy to hear a person's ritual need. First, *the ritual planner must resist any tendency to project her own pain, experience, need, or desire onto the focal person.* This is a real risk, because another's pain can reveal to us our own vulnerability, and our empathy can (inadvertently) draw us back to our own needs and situation.

Second, *a ritual maker must resist any temptation to take as "fact" judgments focal persons may make about themselves or that their family may make about them.* Rather, the ritual maker acknowledges a focal person's self-judgment or reputation as a perspective to be celebrated or healed out of the loving forgiveness through which God sees persons. Indeed, a ritual maker must be careful never to take on a judgment about a person, even if it seems to be a judgment accepted by "everyone." If unable to "see" a focal person from the loving perspective of God's wider vision of creation and redemption, a ritual maker must decline to lead a rite for that focal person. This is part of the spirituality of rite making. Creative ritual is freeing partly because God's wider redemptive truth can be revealed through the ritual's recontextualization of meaning, its mediation of God's love and forgiveness, and its invitation to participate in God's ongoing redemption of the person into life and freedom.

Third, *it would be essential that people leading the planning for a rite of passage or healing for another be able and willing to give themselves over to care for the focal person without one's own needs getting in the way.* Not everyone has a gift of empathy, and for some its necessary cultivation comes harder than for others. Further, as James Fowler points out in his faith-development stages, not everyone has the ability to take the perspective of another, to step out of one's own life-needs and "feel with"—either sympathize or empathize—the pain of another.[24] Megory Anderson's lovely book *Sacred Dying: Creating Rituals for Embracing the End of Life* expresses just how important, yet how difficult, this distance and perspective is:

> *Sacred Dying*'s most important role is taking the attention from those survivors who are going through grief and loss and placing it onto the person who is at the point of death. The focus here is on the dying experience itself, as the last of life's great transitions. . . . Mourning and grief come for the survivors, regardless. I do not try to diminish the agony of anyone watching a loved one die; it is often the hardest thing we have to face.

[Even so, my] hope is that, in spite of our [own] fears and sadness, we can offer our loved one an opportunity to experience death as it should be, with honor, respect, and sacredness.[25]

Anderson challenges the battle metaphor so often used with the dying: "I'm going to defeat this!" She quotes Penelope Wilcock who appreciates the desire to fight, but writes,

Our [most common] response to the helplessness of others is to take rescuing action, to be the cavalry coming over the hill (and it follows that our response to our own helplessness is shame). . . . This approach breaks down in the spiritual care of dying people and their loved ones. . . . It is they, not we, who are the protagonists in this last act of life. The work of the dying is theirs, not ours. Ours is to travel alongside, as companions on their journey.[26]

Sometimes a rescue is not what's needed, even though it can seem easier to try to "fix the problem" than to be present to another's pain. The result of this perception for the dying and others in vulnerable transitions is that rarely is someone helping the dying person from the person's own perspective. As Anderson points out, "Dying persons usually have very little say in what is going on around them. They become mostly objects to be dealt with. 'What are we going to do now?' family members ask. 'I certainly can't take him home with me; I have a family to take care of' . . ."[27]

What Anderson asserts for rituals at the end of life is true for all life passages (which death is), and all healing rites (which death also can be): that the "sacred dying experience is *for the person dying*—all rituals and observances are for him or her. . . . Loved ones must try to respect the experience of dying, and even if they need to sacrifice their own feelings for the time being, they must try to focus 100 percent on the person who is dying."[28] This is a spiritual practice.

2

Ritual Midwives

Planning and Leading Ritual

🌊 The way is creative ritual. Now, who should pave the third way? Who should be part of creating a rite fitting the person's need and the church's theology? The answer is *a community.* None of us is as smart as all of us, as the saying goes, and ritual work calls for wider wisdom than one person alone can invoke. Making ritual is maieutic—midwifing[1]—and requires at least two or three gathering together in Christ's name.

Engaging a Caring, Competent Community for Ritual Planning

Ritual makers need to understand how ritual works and be committed to enabling all the baptized to grow into the fullness of God's intention for them: holy, God's, Christ-like, Spirit-filled. Building upon the first step of empathic inner seeing to assess someone's ritual need, one then begins the creative process of imagining a new rite that will be theologically and experientially effective by tapping creative and compassionate colleagues.

Community is essential, for Christian worship rites are neither planned nor celebrated alone. Everyone who is baptized into Christ is connected to the ecclesial body, in joy and in need. The Christian life is a life lived in community. Ritual making is an ecclesial action, a communal event, not just in the ritual moment, but also in its preparation as well as in its follow-up. In Joanie and Frank's ritual, only six people were present, and others were involved in planning and preparing, but their four witnesses represented many others who also cared for Joanie and Frank. Even in a rite of confession, or communion in a hospital room, when there are only two people present the church is still there, represented by the two people who come in good faith and intention to fulfill the Christian covenant.

Joanie's first act was to call two friends she trusted, who, with their husbands, were also members of her church and who agreed to participate with her. She also called me, an out-of-town consultant she trusted who had experience, to be a resource in thinking it through. Joanie instinctively understood this communal principle: that as one body, the church acts *together* and *on each other's behalf*, and so she reached out to others first. Her instinct was formed in the faith where both identity and ministry arise out of community. Jesus sent the disciples off two by two (Mark 6:7; Luke 10:1). It is as a people that God saves us, not as isolated individuals. The Godhead itself is a community: a Trinity of persons in relationship as one. And in the case of creating rituals, the stakes are too high to do it alone. The work of making a healing ritual is the work of the church, and is done by more than one person, acting in unity on behalf of both the focal person and the body of Christ.

Finding compassionate, competent partners who would understand about acting on the focal person's behalf, and who would collaborate without inserting their own needs or agenda into the process, is therefore a very important principle in planning for creative ritual. The norm for planning any kind of Christian worship is the involvement of several people. Indeed, planning worship is not a one-person operation. One person cannot take enough perspectives to see and plan the whole. One person cannot have enough empathy to imagine every person and every situation needing attention. Worship is prayer by the church, and planning to enable the people of God to encounter the Holy One requires prayer by two or three gathering with Christ in their midst (Matt. 18:20).

When a pastor plans Sunday worship, for example, even if she or he does it alone, the planning is still done in conversation with the author of the lectionary, the authors of the books of worship or prayer books across the centuries, the composers of the music, writers of Internet articles, and others. And even if planned "alone," each instance of Sunday worship is one in a pattern of weekly gatherings for which each denomination and each pastor has a rhythm, a pattern from last week, and personal experience upon which to draw. The planner and the process of planning are steeped in a matrix of Scripture, tradition, denominational theologies, ecclesial practices, local resources, and care for community. One does not begin from scratch.

It is different when generating a rite for which there is no pattern. There are no silent conversation partners who prepared the lectionary, worship books, worship resources, or ordo (typical order of worship). Even though one may sense a deep structure to worship—telling the story, embodying a response, saying a prayer, making music—even these basic elements will vary widely by culture and context. And without cultural or ecclesial templates to follow, it all must be prepared afresh. It takes more than one person to do this.

Although such customized rituals for particular situations are increasing, there are still relatively few well-known instances, and so it is difficult for some to imagine what kind of rituals a planning group would do. Divorce is an obvious example of a common situation needing ritual for both healing and transition, but it is far from the only one. There are many particular situations rare enough not to have a standard rite in a worship book: miscarriage, entering an ecumenical monastic community, discerning a call to serve in (and thus seek) public office, affirmation by one's church to begin a new, nonordained ministry, healing of blindness or other illness, revisiting a site where one was stationed in armed services, preparing to visit for the first time one's birth child or parent who has made contact to seek a relationship, honoring the death of a pet.[2] In places where land is insufficient for burying a person in perpetuity, a rite is needed for the unearthing of the remains of a loved one, and their reinterment somewhere else. For these and hundreds of other ritual needs with little or no history, for which there are meager or no patterns established, where few have walked the path before you—or even *seen* the path—in these generative cases, it is important to work with a caring and knowledgeable group of people who will think, pray, and plan the ritual together.[3] Sometimes members of the planning community may be present through telephone or e-mail, as in Joanie's case. An optimum planning-group size is four or five people, minimally three.

Patricia's situation illustrates how a planning conversation group would work. Patricia had been abused by a clergyman, and after years of therapy, retreats, and inner work, she was still struggling to connect with church.[4] Her ritually sensitive church friend, Chloe, recognized that a rite could help Patricia bridge the final chasm. She asked Patricia whether she would be open to a ritual that would be a kind of purification, to help her complete the healing and put the pain behind her, to free her to no longer feel tainted or shamed by that devastating past. After considering Chloe's unexpected idea, Patricia embraced it, though was unsure how to proceed. Chloe invited her to think of two other women she trusted whom she'd like to help plan it with her. The four women then met weekly for a month, listening to Patricia's story, journals, and dreams, and imagining together what might be included in a rite. At last, the final planning meeting was held, but only with the three midwife-planners. They asked Patricia not to come to this last session in order to help her release her role as "planner" to become solely the rite's "focal person" who would be the subject of the ritual action. This final preparation without Patricia enabled a few gentle surprises to be incorporated, but most importantly, made it clear that the ritual itself is a gift. Patricia's role for that day would be receiver and focal person, not leader of the rite. But the main planning had been done together, with ideas and modifications stimulating, revising, and completing each other. Collegial participation is an important part of ritual planning and enacting.

Four Attributes Necessary for Ritual Planning

Who is this group of people who will plan a rite? It is important to include persons who bring to the table one or more of four attributes: pastoral sensitivity, theological awareness, ethical acuity, and ecclesial connection.[5] These cords, glued together with the art of leading ritual, make up the rope of ritual competence.

Pastoral sensitivity refers to loving the focal person(s), caring for and committing to the focal person's own best interest, and a willingness to give oneself for this person's well-being. Pastoral sensitivity also refers to understanding how human persons operate spiritually, emotionally, and mentally, so as to recognize the process of healing or passage (change) in the other and to facilitate it. Such sensitivity also requires a certain level of maturity, so as to have psychic and emotional boundaries to distinguish one's own issues from the focal person's; self-knowledge; tolerance for another's pain; tolerance for bearing and sustaining creative tension while change takes place; and other skills and knowledge that come with individuation and maturity.

Pastoral sensitivity includes integrity, keeping confidence, and trust with the planning group and focal person. It of course includes compassion. An ability to see what is fitting to invite the focal person into and what is not, as well as which people are fitting to include in a ritual and which are not, is also essential. Such wisdom and sensitivity are needed in the planning group to keep the focus on the focal person, to enable a high level of trust, and to sustain needed ritual intimacy during the rite.

Theological awareness means being conversant with basic Christian understandings of who God is and how God works, what incarnation means and how it shifts the context of our lives, and the rhythm of human life through which God has moved to save and redeem us (that is, creation, sin, judgment, redemption). Other basic understandings are also needed: sacramentality and how God uses the material world to mediate the spiritual,[6] what creation is, what it means to be human, and the power of the paschal mystery to give life. The ability to engage in theological reflection, to see gaps between what Christians believe and how they act, and to recognize both the continuity and the rupture between the culture and the call of the Gospel are needed to keep a ritual grounded in the Holy Trinity and are enabling of the ministry of participants. Theological awareness is essential in the planning in order to have confidence that the resulting ritual will be Christian.

Ethical acuity refers to a working comprehension of the relationship between liturgy and the Christian moral life, including the cultivation of spiritual virtues, dispositions and affections of the heart, and other aspects of character development.[7] The great rhythms of worship are giving, receiving, thanksgiving, inviting, participating, and acting on behalf of. There is not room here to address all the ritual ways worshipers are oriented to God through Christ in the Spirit who forms their very identity as human moral beings. A few factors, however, may serve as a way in to ritual ethical acuity. The first four apply to worship in general, and the others specifically to personal creative rituals—worship in the particular.

First, the creative, caring rituals of healing and transition discussed here *address the God of heaven and earth as their primary referent*. The regular Sunday worship of this God by the community of faith, along with the celebration of Holy Baptism and Holy Communion, is the secondary referent. These rites do not stand alone, but are part of a liturgical ethical matrix of Christian living and intend to widen and deepen the integrity of that lived Christian experience.

Second, the unity and beauty of any rite is part of its ethical shape, because God is One and God is Beauty. Those who serve as ritual midwives for the Spirit's healing, transforming work, therefore, will *attend to integrity in word, action, and sign* as they are choreographed for ritual action.[8]

Third, rituals embody spirit, and Christian rites, offered in Christ by the Spirit, are intended to *mediate the Holy Spirit.* This requires that the spirit of the planners and leaders have integrity. Prayer invoking the Holy Spirit in advance is essential. Because anxiety can shift a focus from the vulnerable person seeking healing and wholeness to a nervous leader, it can be an ethical step to plan a literal or virtual walk-through, rehearsing cues and roles, so that the rite itself can be oriented to God, focused on the person, and open to the Spirit. Doing the rite is finally not the point; it is the doing of it in the integrity of the One who arouses our praise and thanks, calls us to covenant, and impels us to care for each other's spiritual growth. As Don Saliers puts it, "It is certainly not enough that liturgical activities are done, especially if they are done without making our human life vulnerable to the mystery [that is, the Spirit] of God."[9]

A fourth ethical rule of Christian worship is *never put words into worshipers' mouths or actions into worshipers' bodies that they would not be able, for any reason, to say or do with integrity.* This ethic requires monitoring the words of any prayer or responsive reading to be sure they are broadly true enough that any unexpected Christian worshiper who arrived that morning from anywhere on the planet could honestly and robustly proclaim with everyone else. Christian worship in the free context of North America is a public matter, and prayers are offered on behalf of all the worshipers. If the leader intends to pray on behalf of the people, but prays narrow prayers that not everyone can affirm, the pastor has pulled some persons from prayerful, vulnerable openness in the Spirit to analytical critique and closed defensiveness. This divides the body instead of building it up (see 1 Cor. 12; 11:27-29). Wedding vows are always discussed in advance of the ceremony for this same reason. No surprises. People are invited to "full, conscious, and active participation" in rites for them and for others.[10] They need to trust the rite and the leaders to know what will happen, to have a chance to prepare themselves, and to expect to be able to participate fully in the whole worship service.

Fifth, creative ritual is an *act of love offered freely*, and accepted freely, in Christ. There must be no manipulation, no coercion, no pushing of someone into ritual involvement. It is important that they know in advance most of what will happen (except for a few gentle, benevolent surprises in some cases), so that they will be able to participate with confidence and trust (or decline the offer of a ritual). "Jesus means freedom,"[11] and any ritual not freely requested, freely offered, freely received, and freely entered into, would be unfitting to the Gospel and must be declined.

A final ethical point is that creative rituals refer to a great story and the community behind it, so that such rites are both radically particular and ecclesially connected. The roles are representative ones, and ritual *leaders and witnesses need to be conscious of acting on behalf* of the wider church.

Ecclesial connection means assuring that the ritual is not out on its own, but is embedded in the life of the denomination or congregation. The planning group would include someone who is able to represent the church, the body of Christ, through a position (for example, pastor, lay leader, education director, youth minister), through theological education, or by one's personal spiritual depth as recognized and trusted by others (for example, long-time member, elder, beloved teacher). Additionally, a ritual can be ecclesially connected by meeting in a church house or other consecrated space, and also by informing certain pastoral authorities, even if they are not invited to participate. The congregation can be invited to pray in solidarity with those planning and conducting the ritual by placing the focal person's concern in the prayers of the people or the pastoral prayer. Finding intentional and sensitive ecclesial connections is a key part of ritual planning.

The question of ecclesial connection is important and bears on the very impetus to conduct rituals of passage and healing. Much of the groundwork of creative ritual has been laid by persons who were not permitted to represent the institutional church, namely, *women*. Yet aside from denominational polities and hierarchies, the organic need for caring ritual has tended to arise from women's experience, as women have been the locus of domestic ritual and often have highly developed senses of pastoral sensitivity and ritual authority. Women-church[12] was an early invitation to women to provide for themselves the rituals they needed, and to claim the ritual authority to do so. Over the years, women's rituals have been conducted with grace and power, with pastoral and theological insight, and with high experiential effectiveness. This women's work has created a space for experimentation in creative ritual, largely by Roman Catholic women who have been formed in deep liturgical intuition through years of embodied practice.[13] My own hope is to bring this wisdom and care into the wider church; not to remove it from its creative development at the margins, but to awaken the mainstream to its importance and its need.

The ecclesial connection in the women's liturgy movement has been made by the women themselves who are faithful to the One who creates and redeems, thus representing the body of Christ by their faithfulness. Specifically in these women's liturgies, the ecclesial connection is *not* made by a person with institutional position. For example, because women are neither included nor permitted among the ecclesiastical hierarchy of the Roman Catholic Church (among others) in the denomination's current polity, ordained women clergy cannot accomplish the specific rituals needed for women and by women. Women's ways of worship[14] have been self-generated; and because of the inherently human basis for ritual as well as the years of steeping in liturgy that Roman Catholic women have experienced, the rituals generated are typically quite experientially effective. They are specifically not theologically effective in certain ways, since their very performance is a critique of theological doctrines that deny ritual authority to women. Rather, building on their cultic memory of pastoral liturgy, the conducting of effective rituals for one another has cultivated ritual competence and authority, and provided a standpoint from which to challenge official structures that deny the same to women. The ritual knowledge so generated, however, is a gift to the whole church. Ecclesial connection may be made through faithful Christian witness or ritual fluency and competence or symbolic valence or official position or by other relationships with ecclesial bodies.

Thus ecclesial connection raises the issue of authority as well as symbolic representation: Who may, and who can, represent the churches? The response to these issues has widened since World War II through both the women's liturgy movement and the lay ministry movement. The latter movement also seeks to invert ecclesial power so that the baptized will understand themselves as the primary servants of God and claim authority for ethical service in the world. Both movements assert that persons other than ordained clergy can indeed represent the *ecclesia* symbolically in such pastoral ritual-planning groups. The important factor is the ritual competence of the person, not his or her official or sacramental status. Persons' symbolic valence is important. Sometimes persons with the authority of a position, such as licensure, certification, or ordination, should specifically not be invited. Sometimes they specifically should be. Sometimes a strong symbolic presence may be needed for the planning of a particular ritual action.

When Chloe invited Patricia to select two other women for the planning group, she set the stage for pastoral sensitivity, since Patricia would not invite anyone she did not trust. Chloe had the pastoral sensitivity to recognize the ritual need in the first place, so the committee was assured of this skill. Yet both Chloe and one of the other women were ecclesially connected (though not ordained), and quietly let the trusted pastor know what was happening as they reserved space in the church house, both for the planning meetings and for the ritual. Chloe herself was the most theologically aware, and by making contact with the pastor, she had a doorway for additional theological input if needed. All the women were ethically strong, but again, Chloe best understood the relationship between ethics and ritual and thus assured that all these attributes were borne by at least one person.

Roles Necessary to Planning a Ritual

So how would one put together a planning team? Knowing that the pastoral, theological, ethical, and ecclesial strands are needed in the conversation, who might typically represent these four attributes and also have trusted and caring relationships with the focal person? Because planning groups meet for differing lengths of time, availability may be a factor: sometimes persons may participate in the first part of the process, and others may join later. Foundationally, however, making sure there are persons with the four attributes, a planning group includes the focal persons (at least at first), persons who know and love them and can see the relationship of the rite to the persons' ongoing growth into Christ through baptismal ministry, and persons who represent the family of faith. Each of these will be addressed in turn.

Because a ritual is a free gift offered for the well-being of focal persons who are suffering or in transition, the first persons involved in the beginning of the planning process are *the focal persons.* Even when rituals are highly celebrative, they are not surprise parties, and they must never be given unexpectedly. Ideally, each focal person would be involved in planning. Sometimes, this is not possible or a person is reluctant. But Christian rituals are not manipulative, nor is there a *disciplina arcani* in which rites are kept secret, either from the public or from those preparing for initiation. A few unexpected delights may show up in the rite, of course, in the form of gifts to the focal persons, or in an unexpected gift of the Spirit. But if one person desires to have a rite in order to accomplish something in relationship to another person without telling the person in advance, you must gently but firmly reject this idea. In the case of Joanie, her first conversation was with Frank, the other focal person. He agreed to participate, but not to plan. His wishes were honored. Yet if, as in this case, it is not possible for a focal person to be part of the planning, the leader as well as all the other planners must attend to and speak up for the best interest of the focal person who is absent.

The planning process also would necessarily include *one or more persons with deep trust, closeness, compassion for and understanding of* the focal persons, in order to care for the focal persons' own best interest, desire their spiritual wholeness, and empathize with their circumstances through this process. A ritual is itself a gift. It is a process of lovingkindness. It takes time and effort, given not out of duty but freely, out of compassion. Therefore, persons with wisdom, ritual fluency, love, compassion, and understanding of the focal person are needed to plan it.[15] Creative ritual is not only for the simple care of a sibling in Christ, but also to help her or him become all she or he was created to be. Someone who recognizes not only the immediate need of the person, but also the larger baptismal context of this situation as part of the focal person's continuing journey into God manifested in ministry is needed on the planning committee.

Finally, at least one ecclesial leader (other than the focal person) will serve as *representative of the family of faith*. In some cases, this will be an official person, such as a clergyperson or a committee chair. In other cases it will be someone connected to the church and its leaders, perhaps friends or theologians or caring persons who can speak for the needs of the focal person. This may also be the person who recognizes how this event fits into the focal person's process of baptismal living or the congregation's baptismal life.

But sometimes there cannot be a planning committee at all. Sometimes the denomination's polity or theology will not support what is needed for the person's healing. For example, a gathering of healing and passage around divorce may not occur in some denominations' conse-crated spaces. Some pastors would find themselves under interdiction if they presided over or even witnessed a covenantal union between two people who were not being legally married, such as elderly life compan-ions or same-sex couples. However, if marriage is not possible or a pastor may not be present or it is not possible for this church to offer the caring ritual needed, then pastors are obligated to refer the person(s) to another congregation or denomination that may be able to provide the care needed. Churches must uphold their doctrines, but without ever denying care for the vulnerability of the people who come to the church to place their need before the Lord. In either case, whether preparing a ritual or referring persons to other parts of the church for caring ritual, the pastor is acting on behalf of the body of Christ. And this is the baptismal call.

Roles Necessary to Conducting a Ritual

In addition to the skills persons bring to the planning group, there are also roles to be filled in conducting the rite itself. Whether or not mem-bers of the planning group are to fill these ritual roles, carefully planning how each role will be fulfilled in the rite is important. At least four roles are needed during a Christian ritual: focal person(s), ritual leader, body of Christ, and witness. Each of these distinct ritual roles will be described and exemplified.

1. The *focal person* is the particular person for whom the rite is done. In most cases, it is obvious who the focal person is. In the divorce ritual, the focal persons are Joanie and Frank. It's the retiree, the birthday girl, the one being baptized, the one dying, the one moving. It's the one mak-ing the change, the one being celebrated. It's the one needing healing or facing transition, the one with the miscarriage, the one just diagnosed with progressive dementia.

Sometimes, however, it's not so obvious who the focal person is. There may be several vulnerable people. Can the rite be for more than one? Often not. Ritual makers must, as part of their fluency and compe-tence, pay attention and clearly name whom the rite will focus on so that it can be oriented toward *that person's* perspective.

For example, it is essential to allow the dying person to be focal even though the family also feels vulnerable. I remember a man who took his weak cat to the veterinarian, and the prognosis was that she would likely be put down during the week. The man was inconsolable, so much so that he had become absorbed in his proleptic grief, and had not been to see the animal. "I can't bear to face her," he said. The cat, however, was not only weak, in pain, and at the end of life, but was now also abandoned at this tenuous and vulnerable juncture. When the man came to himself and realized how much she needed him, his own distress abated, and he was able to accompany her through to the end. The same applies to people we love.

Sometimes there are two focal persons, and the ritual maker must discern whether it will work to honor both needs in one rite, or whether two rites are more fitting. For instance, the deceased person is focal at a funeral, and for this pastoral-theological reason the person's body is always accompanied, is met at the door of the church, others sit vigil with it during the night, and words of thanks and honor about the person are spoken at the funeral. Of course, the grievers are also focal. Most funerals are pretty good at honoring both the focal person (deceased) and the focal group (mourners).[16] But for religions that honor the body, such as Judaism and Christianity (and because Christianity is an incarnational religion), if an emphasis has to be chosen, it is essential to honor the deceased. Another rite can always be created for the living, if needed.

An example of creating two rites, for the deceased and for the mourners, comes from the Alaskan Athabaskan Indians, who have solved this problem creatively. In their culture, a *memorial potlatch* is held at the time of the first anniversary of the person's death in Christian villages. Traditionally, since before Christianity, the potlatch would last several days and people would come from villages up- and down-river to celebrate. A memorial song would be written about the deceased person. The person's family will have spent all year preparing for a great *giveaway,* sharing all the deceased's belongings with other villagers and guests, as well as making additional gifts to give away. While both the funeral and the memorial potlatch honor the deceased and the mourners, the funeral is particularly focused on the deceased, while the memorial potlatch is particularly focused on the grieving family.[17]

This is important to mention because as cremation becomes more common and the demand of burial is not imminent, it is possible to put off a ritual for several months or even years. One pastor was shocked in his new congregation to have a family come with Grandma's ashes to plan a "funeral," and request chances for the grandchildren to each have a moment to offer a special talent. This did not suggest the tone of mourning and sadness that typified most funeral planning. Then it came out that Grandma had died ten months before, and they were just gathering the family together. The family was orienting toward each other as focal. There is certainly a place for this, as the Alaskan potlatches show. However, what was missing was the service in which Grandma was focal, so that she could be committed to God and her body carried to her final resting place.

The wonder of caring ritual is that it is creative and personal. And there is no statute of limitations. But too often, there is no ritual, or a key focal person is neglected. Sometimes, there is no community of ritual midwives to provide a ritual, and all are left on their own to cope with the tear in the fabric of life.

2. The second role essential for conducting a rite is that of *ritual leader*, shaman, master of ceremony, priest, pastor. Sometimes one can identify the ritual leader as the one who is "up front," the visible one, conducting the action. Other times, the ritual leader is more like the stage manager, helping everything happen beautifully and in sequence and in the right spirit, but from behind the scenes. The ritual leader may participate to a certain extent in the action, but the leader's role is to enable the focal person and the other participants to receive the experience of the rite.

Poet Samuel Taylor Coleridge referred to what happens to the audience of a play as the "willing suspension of disbelief"—that is, entering a covenant to set aside one's meta-awareness of how the effects are created in order to enter into the immediacy of the dramatic action. In ritual action, this is the trait described earlier as operating below the conscious level (Bell's "misrecognition"). For this to occur for the participants, someone needs to be quite conscious of timing, sequence, and cues, and to pay close attention to what is occurring for the focal person. This conscious person (who is *not* suspending disbelief) is the ritual leader.

It is apparent, then, that one of the basic pastoral as well as practical truths of creative ritual making is that *the focal person and the ritual leader are not the same person*. It is essential to separate these roles in order for the focal persons to receive what the rite intends. This principle must be emphasized because often focal persons are so involved in planning the rite that they are inclined to keep planning and directing even as the rite begins. But then they are unable to receive the full effect of the rite.

Focal persons have a vested and very personal interest in the ritual and are glad to do much of the preliminary work (for example, contact the people, order the flowers, select the readings). If the authority for enabling the rite to occur falls only to focal persons, however, the divided mind of running the show and receiving the gift will necessarily be in conflict. It is important that there be a ritual leader to manage the operation of the event and to free focal persons to trust that all will be well, so that they can relax and tune in to the immediacy of the power, grace, and Spirit in the ritual. The ritual itself is a gift, and focal persons are cared for, among other things, by receiving its effects. If they are in charge, receiving the gift is not possible in the same way. This separation of roles can easily occur if someone else offers to make a rite, or if the focal person asks someone to do so (and is then willing to let the leader lead).

Not only might focal persons try to direct the rite, but there is also a challenge for the ritual leader. Because some of the same skills that enable a person to be comfortable speaking "up front" also appeal to the ego, the leader may be tempted to impose an agenda, or quit listening to the Spirit, or simply take over (with the best of intentions, of course). But the rite is not about the ritual leader. The rite is about the focal person. And indeed, the leader is a servant leader, and must commit to the deep heart-listening that will not seek to control or to create outcome, but to engender cooperatively a worshipful structure that will give much space for the Spirit's movement to care for the focal person.

3. The third role in conducting a rite is those who represent the *body of Christ*. Rite makers must be aware that although focused on one or more persons, a Christian ritual is always offered to the glory of God, and thereby also touches many persons even beyond those present at the rite itself. Rituals are powerful for the very reason that they are bigger than any one person (that is, Bell's "redemptive hegemony").

For example, sometimes those present at the rite as support and witnesses may receive as much from the ritual as the focal person. Or rites can spill over beyond themselves: one woman shared how moved she was just walking by a chapel during worship when she heard the beautiful sound of a cappella singing, and how that had been a word from God to her that day. To realize that a rite may represent and affect more than we know is humbling and presses us to excellence.

Since a ritual for one person affects many people and is done on behalf of the wider ecclesial community, it is important that someone be present at the rite itself who represents the church, the body of Christ. Who should these ecclesial persons be? It makes symbolic sense to invite trusted members of the congregation who matter to the focal person to serve as witnesses. One might also invite church persons with a certain expertise, symbolic valence, reputation, or pastoral skill to be present on behalf of the *ecclesia.* Persons with officially designated authority are often included. And persons who will give themselves in prayer prior to the ritual might be also invited to the rite itself.

If appropriate to invite persons from other denominations, the body of Christ is more strongly represented. A blessed side effect of such invitations can be community caring and learning and even spiritual transformation.

And in addition to those specifically invited, the ritual leader will usually also represent the church. The leader holds open the spiritual space for the work of the Holy Spirit while also managing the ritual action, tending the focal person, and assuring that others present are enabled to participate. Seeking excellence down to details while holding the ritual action lightly in the Spirit is a skill and an art. It works best if the details have been worked out in the planning: How will all the participants be engaged? What will cue each step of the sequence? If the advanced work is careful, then the leader can conduct the ritual lightly in prayer while paying attention to the Spirit's working. The results of good ritual come both as gift from God and from careful attention by the leader and/or participants. A healing rite builds up the body of Christ. It enables a person and his or her situation to be contextualized in the cosmic context of God's loving creation and redemption and thus become part of salvation history.

It is a good idea before a ritual begins for leaders to enter into a prayer state and release unto God the planning, rite, focal person, and other participants, shifting away from human effort to God's action. I often remember the empty chair at the Jewish seder for Elijah, the greatest prophet, in case he should come that evening—a sign of openness to the divine work, which is the real work at hand. Remembering the divine meaning and context helps leaders stay open to the Spirit's movement and assures decisions are not overly narrow while strengthening the whole ecclesial body. It also lends a certain gravitas and solemnity to the event for the focal person, the leader, and the others who attend: the witnesses.

4. The fourth necessary ritual role is that of *witness.* Sometimes a person may bear dual roles, such as serving both as witness and as

representative of the body of Christ. But I list them separately to clarify that though it may be one person, it is still two roles.

Eyewitnesses are central in the Bible to the spreading of the gospel. Eyewitnesses continue to be central in our own age as verification of what really happened. Videos are an extension of eyewitnessing, although they are inferior because they give only a shallow or "thin" view of what went on: a meaningful or "thick" description can only be given by a human being who is present in the context and can feel the difference, for example, between a grimace and a sincere smile or between a wave of dismissal and an intentional wave of farewell.[18]

Not only as eyewitness, the third party to an event makes the event "real" through the perspective he or she offers, as well as the neutrality of role. Inasmuch as the focal person, ritual leader, and ecclesial representative are involved in the action as principals in the event's meaning, the nonprincipal witnesses generally have no investment in any particular symbolic action except to care about the focal person and that the ritual will successfully effect what is desired. Thus focal persons are enabled to see what is happening to themselves through the perspective of the witnesses.[19]

Jesus said, "Where two or three are gathered together in my name, there am I in the midst of them" (Matt. 18:20). Sometimes there are just two (such as in a rite of confession), and then the ritual leader doubles as the witness, and the two together represent the body of Christ. In most cases, the witnesses are other persons. Even in a private wedding, for instance, there would be the pastor or justice of the peace, the focal couple, and at least one witness. Some weddings have hundreds of witnesses, in which case two attendants are designated to represent all the witnesses in signing the marriage license.

In an ecclesial rite, all who attend represent the rest who could not. In this way the witnesses are present for themselves and for the focal persons, but they are also present on behalf of those who could not come. It's disappointing to miss a wedding or a funeral, but as long as *someone* is there, there is a completeness to the community as well as to the ritual event. Ritual participants bear roles on behalf of the body of Christ, so that when they speak and stand and pray, they are not acting privately on their own. They participate on behalf of the whole *ecclesia*. Because this is such an important awareness for ritual participants, we now look at what it means to act on behalf of others.

Speaking or Acting "On Behalf Of"

Once an appropriate group of people is gathered to plan the ritual, it will be important to recognize that they are not just acting for themselves. Rather, they have come together on behalf of Christ and his body, the church. It is important to understand the principle of acting on behalf of one another so as not to forget that it is God who has called them together. In order to do that, you have to be part of a community. And when you are, you take on a certain responsibility for the ethics and ethos (or spirit) of that community and you participate (more or less) in mediating that ethos and ethic both within the group and to outsiders. Different communities (families, organizations, crowds, and so on) have different spirits, tones, assumptions, orientations, or attitudes.[20]

Consciously aware or not, a person stands for her or his community, and thus can be tainted or shamed when the community acts inappropriately, as well as be honored or gratified when their community acts honorably. A person is an individual, but never only an individual. A person does not cease being an individual when part of a community. Each person also receives and manifests the spirit of the community. There is a symbolic connection between a group and its members so that any member may be perceived as a symbol of the group. Thus it is possible for persons to act for themselves, but also to represent the community, intentionally or not. Both are true.

The Christian community is a community conscious of being created, redeemed, and sustained by the Holy Trinity. It seeks to be made holy in order to be worthy of its identity, but also in order to be able to carry out its holy work. Thus when people gather together as the church, it is the Holy Spirit who sings and loves and works in the community's midst. Experiences of the presence of the Holy Spirit both manifest and enable the church to be itself and to carry out Christ's ministry.

When people see Christians in worship or in action, each Christian person or congregation acts on behalf of all, consciously or not. Gandhi, deeply moved by his reading of the Bible, visited a Christian congregation on a Sunday; but when that community turned Gandhi away because he was "colored," he inferred something about "the Christian people" who were not living their Scripture, and he decided to stay a Hindu. For Gandhi that day, one congregation represented the church. Sadly, however, the people in that congregation likely never realized that they were representing not only themselves, but the whole Christian family, and

that their prejudice that day besmirched the name of Christianity for a
generation of people.

From the other perspective, people may assume a person is representing a group she does not intend to represent simply by associating
her with groups of which they perceive her to be part. When Mother
Teresa spoke, people received her message, but some also drew inferences
about nuns and about the Roman Catholic Church (more appropriate),
others perhaps about women or short people (less appropriate). When
Barack Obama ran for U.S. President, different people experienced him
as representing different things: men, black men, community developers,
constitutional lawyers, people with Arab or African names, children of
single mothers, unabashed Christians, intelligent rhetoricians, and so on.
The nature of human personhood is both that we are ourselves, unique,
particular, and that we are part of a whole which we affect and by which
we are affected.

A significant result of consciously acting on behalf of a group is that a
sense of community or unity is created; an experience of oneness, of being
part of one another is realized. This includes the sense of being part of
something greater than oneself, which is a core human spiritual need (and
the basis for all the covenants in Scripture, including Abram's response
to God's invitation to be the leader of a people in covenant with God; cf.
Gen. 12:1-9). More than this, one gains a sense of belonging essential to
humans: knowing one is not alone, trusting in others, sharing in a common purpose.

Consequences of such communal experience can be gratifying or
shameful. If the collective group I'm a part of does something wonderful,
though I myself may have had nothing to do with it directly and so cannot take credit for it, I will enjoy the celebration of what we did together,
and I will experience joy and gratification: we are all honored. Conversely,
if our group does something wrong or unethical, small or hurtful, we are
all dishonored and each may experience shame.

This ethical covenantal commitment is built right into the baptismal
covenant. Christians united to Christ in death and resurrection enter the
moral obligation to act uprightly on behalf of the body of Christ as well
as the voiceless, the poor and hungry, the sick and imprisoned (Matt.
25:31-46). Even more, as a "royal priesthood" (1 Pet. 2:9-10), the people
covenanted to God in Christ are called to love and serve the world on
behalf of God (as Christ did), and to bring the concerns of the world

before God in prayer (as Christ did).[21] Christians are called to witness on behalf of the already-but-not-yet reign of God, to speak on behalf of those who have no voice, to offer hospitality—and caring liturgies—on behalf of the community of faith. To others it may seem risky, and it is, unless those who act and offer are living lives of the utmost integrity and probity. Acting on behalf of others, in all worship including creative ritual, requires moral soundness and holy living. It is bold. But without taking this risk, much life-changing care in the community of faith goes undone.

And besides, there is an ethical imperative in the Christian life, in multiple examples in Scripture, that Christians keep awake to the connections that their lives, actions, and words make to everyone else in the community (and beyond), and that they honor the Christian people's good name by acting honorably on their behalf. The call to act on each other's behalf is scriptural (Acts 2:44, 3:6-12). The biblical word *steward* refers to the great and sacred trust placed upon each member by the Lord, in covenant with the whole body (Matt. 25:14-30, 18:23-35, 21:33-46; 1 Cor. 4:1-2). Those baptized into Christ are part of the one body of Christ and are called to act lovingly and prophetically on behalf of others. Stewardship of ("building up," Eph. 4:29) the body is a moral obligation for everyone who has accepted this covenant and membership in baptism. A ritual-planning group's role, above all, is to serve as steward of both the focal persons in their vulnerability, and of the *ecclesia* who pledge themselves to live as Christ, building one another up into servant leaders for the life of the world.

The ritual-planning community, then, bears a priestly servant role, following Christ who acted on behalf of the people and their vulnerability. Christ himself is understood as the mediator, the one who acts on behalf of those who fall into sin who have promised to love their neighbor and then fail to do so, forgiving them that they might receive new life. The Holy Spirit advocates on behalf of those who love the truth, dwelling within them (John 14:16-17). Christ the Redeemer acted out of deep self-giving love on behalf of humanity's weakness, those problems from which we cannot extricate ourselves. Various atonement theories attempt to describe how it is that Christ's self-giving love on the cross "covers" the sin of all humankind. Describing Karl Barth's approach, one author explains that "Jesus has cried and suffered on our behalf."[22] In Hebrews, Christ is understood as the great high priest, the one who mediates on another's behalf. In 1 Pet. 2:9-10, it is the covenanted body of Christ who are the priestly people, mediating on behalf of the world to God, and on behalf of God to the world. Intercessory prayers fulfill this agency, asking God—on behalf of a world that may not even know God—to love, forgive, heal, transform. Compassion may not exist everywhere, but when one of us speaks a word of compassion, a human being has fulfilled the human role and privilege. Liturgical theologian Louis-Marie Chauvet explains, quoting Pierre Bourdieu,

> An "I promise" has value only as a pact between my partner, myself, and the collectivity which governs the conditions of their validity of promises or as a "relation between the properties of the discourse, the properties of the one who pronounces it, and the properties of the institution that authorizes one to pronounce it." The power of words . . . as a performative ritual manifestation, resides in the fact that they are not pronounced by an individual as an individual, but rather as the proxy of the group, as the *representative* of its *"symbolic capital."*[23]

Leaders and laity often have more symbolic capital than they realize.

In Sunday worship especially, but in all Christian ritual, the relationship of Christians to God in Christ and the Spirit, to one another, and to the world, is practiced or "rehearsed."[24] Ritual action, like medical practice, enables the Christian community to get better and better at paying attention to each other, honoring each other, and eventually risking on behalf of each other. The community comes to experience its identity as the people called by God and pledged to God in baptism, and pledged to build each other up to become more and more like Christ. Living—practicing—this identity in worship makes it more possible to live it outside worship.

Again, this role is biblical. In particular, the sacred trust inherent in an agent who speaks as proxy of the group or acts on behalf of the employer is a frequent theme in Jesus' parables. Called "manager" in the NRSV (Luke 16:1-13), the earlier English word *steward* more clearly describes the trusted agent acting on behalf of and in relationship with another. There are the tenants who rebel against the vineyard owner, to the point of even killing the son (Luke 20:9-19; Matt. 21:33-46). There is the parable of reward for faithful financial stewardship, from which the word *fiduciary* comes (Latin *fiducia* = in faith, confidence, trust), for careful investing on behalf of the one you serve ("pounds," Luke 19:11-27; "talents," Matt. 25:14-30). There is a discourse on careful stewardship in which faithful caring for a little earns the privileged responsibility of stewardship of much (Luke 16:10-12). Generating a Christian ritualization also calls for the role of steward, not of someone else's property, perhaps, but of someone else's emotions and relationships. The ethical imperative includes declining to facilitate a rite if one is unable at the time to carry such a sacred trust, for whatever reason. To say no when appropriate is also to act honorably and on behalf of the community of faith.

In addition to one's own moral integrity, the spiritual disposition or "religious affection"[25] central to the stewardship of Christian ritualization is empathy (from Greek), whose other name is compassion (from Latin). This spiritual, ethical, pastoral sensitivity enables a prospective leader to recognize ritual need—and then, in planning a rite, to "hear" what the proper spirit of the rite needs to be, to tune into the subtleties of history and relationship that must be included for the sake not only of transition, but also of healing and ritual honesty.

What makes acting on behalf of others such an ethical imperative as well as an ethical challenge is that there are risks, and the risks are real. There are those who might imagine they were empathizing, but were actually projecting: they may, with all best intention, assert themselves "on another's behalf" when they do not know the person well enough to speak for them. Every one of us thinks best from our own perspective (after all, who else's perspective do we carry?). And every one of us has the unfortunate potential to name what we think is best for another, and then to act with all caring intentions, only to blindly trample the other person (or other creature) and never notice.

This is a great risk. The human heart is subject to self-deception;[26] and the tendency to absolutize our own viewpoint as "truth" is so natural it has been called "original" sin. Real damage can be done to a person when the one caring is unconscious of this tendency and of her or his personal needs or desires, which can so easily be pressed onto another, who may be vulnerable. The fields of spiritual guidance and pastoral care have labored to establish practices and identify safeguards to prevent these occurrences. Pastoral sensitivity and ethical acuity include such practices for ritual leaders as being in an accountability relationship with a pastor, spiritual director, or psychotherapist, and actively, willingly, doing one's own inner work to assure that when with another, one is able to hear clearly or to know when not able to do so, so as to protect the vulnerable other. The maieutic ritual-making practice is an exercise not in control, but in partnership.

Given this conscious care with one's own inner clarity, and in a relationship where the goal is the other's empowerment, independence, and human maturity, there are fitting times in the Christian community to act in someone's name, on their behalf: to do unto another what you would want them to do for you, if you were they. This is walking in someone else's moccasins so as to understand and honor their perspective and values, from their point of view.

Such empathic agency is easier "caught" than taught. But a community of ritual midwives serves as check and balance on one's empathy and intention to act as good steward on behalf of another. And indeed, if such standing for another or deep compassion is not present, it is better to forgo a rite or to call others to do it than to mediate only part of reality.

Finally, though, the joy and goodness of being part of a covenant community is that the whole community can care through the ones who gather, for the ones present represent the whole. Part of our life as Christians is to be there for one another, and to extend beyond our familiar communities to be there for others—especially those who have no one else, those stuck at a fence without a stile or stranded on the shore without a ship. No one can provide a ritual wholly for him- or herself. For a ritual to happen, someone(s) must not only see the need, but be willing to offer to plan and lead it on behalf of the vulnerable focal persons, on behalf of the persons' friends and family who don't know how to care for them, and on behalf of the church, the *ecclesia*—for Christians on the other side of the world can neither see nor help. We can, because we are here. Each of us is called to act on each other's behalf. We never know when it will be or when the person will be *us*. Let us be vigilant. And let us be faithful; for if not us, then who?

3

Metaphors and Symbols

Linking a Person's Story to the Christian Story

❧ Having named "what" (creative rites) and "who," we now ask "how." The third principle for creating rituals opens up the way symbol and metaphor engender sacramental action so that an intimate bond can be made between the person's own story (need, pain, vulnerability, joy) and the great story of creation and redemption through Christ by the Spirit. The goal is not just doing a ritual as a "product" but, rather, engendering a ritual process. The whole course of creating a rite enables transition and healing. And this process contributes to the "baptismal process," which is the rhythm of living fully into one's baptized life in Christ. We begin with finding a fitting metaphor, which is itself a creative and life-giving process.

Words have power. Poetry mediates meaning that strikes "deeply into the bone."[1] The pen and the sermon are more powerful than the sword inasmuch as they arouse people to see differently and motivate people to change and to act. The art of how to move people's hearts while persuading their minds—*rhetoric*—is an art largely focused on figures of speech. Of late, the generic word for these "figures," words that paint pictures impelling hearers into other worlds, is *metaphor.*

In his book *Deeply into the Bone,* ritual scholar Ronald Grimes encourages readers to venture forth into ritual making, with eyes open to risks, but with awareness also open to the power rituals have to carry persons across initiatory and other passages, including the passage from illness to healing.[2] Metaphors are central to this process. When they are enacted, metaphors "can make us sick or make us well; we *somatize* them, transforming words and images into flesh and bone, heart and gut. . . . One way to define ritual is as the enactment of a metaphor."[3]

Arriving at a "Defining Metaphor"

While Joanie's rite was not a perfect ritual specimen and did not include all six of the principles found here, it was especially, stunningly brilliant in the metaphor Joanie herself identified, a metaphor that became the central action and the central poetry of the rite. Her story illustrates how the right metaphor can define the ritual action and create the symbolic power that can indeed mediate healing and passage. The seed of a defining metaphor was planted in the original soil of Joanie's request for a rite. It turned out to be wide and true enough to connect Joanie and Frank to the wider human story and lead to the ritual's central symbolic action.

In asking for my assistance, Joanie invited me to switch roles, from caring friend to empathic ritual maker, as I had helped dozens of people ritualize times of healing and passage and life turnings. It was clear that this was an extremely vulnerable time for Joanie and Frank, and that they were facing the death of a marriage, a vow, and a way of life. The natural "next step" for Joanie was to figure out "what to do." She wanted to imagine how the ritual would go.

What I have learned through such consultations, however, is that deciding "what to do" comes later. That is, every ritual is an event with a beginning, a middle, and an end. There are words spoken, prayers said; there is movement, and often song; there is a flow from the start to the finish. But in order to decide what words to say, what sequence to use, what action to be performed, one does well first to explore and discern a defining metaphor that can help point toward symbols that would have power for the focal person(s).

Continuing to engage the two principles of empathic listening to Joanie's needs and feelings from her own perspective, and realizing that she would not have to do everything herself (since Grace, David, Barbara, Robert, and I, her community, would be working on Joanie and Frank's behalf), I now turned my creative imagination toward the color, the tonal context, that would be the ritual's matrix. Letting her in on the process, I asked her the first important question about the rite. It was the question about metaphor.

"In order to figure out what to do, the first thing we need to do is discern a defining metaphor for this rite, a strong analogy for what is happening to you and Frank." I began to pose questions, trying to use the thoughts and feelings she had just expressed to me. "What's it like to lose half your home, to wake up in the morning and be faced with signs that he is gone, that you are alone, that the marriage is over? What is it like to let go, to start over, give up years of struggle and commitment to him? What is it like to love someone, to love the children who are yours, and to find yourself no longer a family?"

Then I tried on some examples, thinking out loud with her. "Let's think of nature. Is it like a tree, cut off at the roots? No, because you and he are each still living. Is it like the Army Corps of Engineers dividing a river bed and creating two tributaries? Is it like having your arm cut off? Is it like . . . ?" We struggled with several ideas, none of which seemed to work.

I tried history. "What in history or in Scripture is it like? Is it like the children of Israel, sent into exile, dispersed? Do you feel like the remnant?"

"Yes, in a way," she acknowledged, "although I'm the one staying home. Home will change—but I'm not wandering." "Will Frank be wandering?," I asked, for the rite needed to be effective for both of them. "Not that I know of . . ."

Of course. Frank was operating on thoughts and feelings that Joanie could not understand. And to ask Joanie to imagine what Frank was feeling would separate her from the immediacy of her own experience. Ideally, such a ritual would be planned with both Frank and Joanie. But without Frank's participation in the planning, it was important for me to work with Joanie, because she was the one who was here. The important thing was that the rite be *true*. Liturgy shares a truth with literature, a truth recapitulated in the incarnation: that what is most personal is also the most universal; that in describing quite specifically one reality, a window is opened onto all reality. I trusted that if I could help make this rite true for Joanie, its integrity would carry over to Frank and the others participating in the rite.

We tried on some nursery rhymes, comic strips, the current news. Then I turned to her field—art.

"Let's think of art forms," I tried again. "Is there anything in music that represents the intense loss, the obvious missing parts of your life, the end of a way of living?" We paused. Nothing came to mind. I tried fabric arts. "What about in weaving? This seems like a reverse weaving, a kind of unraveling—"

Suddenly, I heard a sharp intake of breath. "Oh! I know what needs to be sacrificed for this ritual," she breathed. "The dining room tablecloth is woven, with multiple colors in it—more than half a dozen colors. That table is where we shared our family meals. It's where our kids did their homework. It's where we invited guests to dine with us. It's where we had conversations, fights, reconciliations. That table was the center of our life together. And this is truly as if the tablecloth is becoming unraveled."

It was perfect. The table and tablecloth would symbolize the marriage, which was metaphorically becoming unraveled. How well this could express the contraries in this situation: the table of unity and discord, the table of fellowship, and now the table of divorce. And, of course, table suggests eucharistic imagery, the oneness greater than the sum of us—and now, the loss that is also greater than the individuals. The tablecloth, like the marriage, would be no more.

It was Joanie who had recognized this. And now she went on: "I'll start tonight. I'll cut it up in pieces, and unravel all the threads. I'll put them in piles. It's as though there'll be a pile for our daughter—maybe the red threads—and one for our son—the green; a mound of threads for Frank, one for me, and others for friends, guests, family." This would be a labor. And labor is needed both for anything to die, and also for anything new to be born.

"It will be hard work, Joanie. Will you do it all yourself?"

"I may get people to help me, during the week. I have several meetings." This, too, would be just right, I thought. Others could labor with her, midwife her by hearing her story. She would not be alone, and this work together would help prepare for the rite, help prepare her to live an unmarried life, and help in her healing. "Save the last bit to do on Saturday, together," I advised. "Let the completion of the unraveling be the enacted symbol in your ritual." She agreed.

Our goal for the ongoing life of Christian faith is to help people flow ever more deeply into Christ in order to live their baptismal covenant. Our method is to notice where the flow is stopped, and to (1) discern whether there may be a ritual need, and (2) gather a planning group. Now, seeking how to create a caring rite, we (3) engage theological imagination around the focal person's thoughts and feelings to find a viable metaphor to express the situation's complexity in a central symbolic action for the ritual. For Joanie, the metaphor of unraveling seemed that it could carry the meaning of the death of the marriage. We would then need to work the metaphor to create a bridge to new life.

How Metaphor Works

The word *metaphor* is a Greek term meaning a conveyance or vehicle. A metaphor "carries" one idea by means of another. The idea of a transcendent meaning being carried or borne is manifest in the traditional understanding of "sacrament" as made up of some "thing"—usually large and mysterious (like God's grace, or movement of the Spirit)—called in Latin *res* (= "thing"), and the more accessible sign of the thing, in Latin *signum* (= "sign"). In this, insight is given into the less known by comparison with a more known. "A mighty fortress is our God" compares God (a lesser known, great mystery) to something tangible and better known: a mighty fortress. This line from Martin Luther's hymn text, an interpretation of Psalm 46, does what all metaphor does: it both reveals and conceals aspects of a reality.[4] To enter the world of the metaphor and look quite literally at God as mighty fortress, God is revealed as strong, protective, sturdy, encompassing, embracing what is within, standing firm, and also impenetrable, opaque, large. At the same time, other attributes of God are concealed in this metaphor, such as God's gentle tenderness, mercy, and forgiveness, and God as teacher, leader, and judge. No metaphor can communicate the whole of another reality. But each metaphor can reveal the depth of one facet; and with multiple metaphors, more and more of the sparkle may come alive.

Thus metaphor reveals complex reality in a simple, vibrant, memorable way. In addition to comparing a less known to a more known, a metaphor may overlay two unlikes, revealing things about each (and also not revealing other things). New and multivalent meanings are created that can continue to unfold in the human heart and memory for years. Paul Ricoeur calls this a *surplus of meaning.*[5]

A metaphor is especially valuable in a ritual for four reasons. First, it carries a multiplicity of meanings—even contrasting meanings—all at once (such as a fragrant, heavenly scented rose is beautiful to look at, but also has prickly thorns). This not only makes the ritual story true and real, but it enables participants to connect with the ritual's meaning and action, each according to her or his own particular life (for example, for some, the thorns may be more true this week than the fragrance).

Second, a metaphor carries not only meanings but an ethos or feeling-tone. One company was ending an operation, and anxious employees began to refer to their plant as a "sinking ship"—until the management shifted the metaphor to "the last voyage," evoking a completely different affective orientation to the change.[6]

Third, by invoking an analogy, metaphor lifts participants out of the narrowness of the specific condition of the ritual and connects them to a broader human experience. Relativizing the particular condition helps the focal persons recognize that their circumstances are not a narrow, personal prison, but are part of the very human condition God redeemed in Christ by the Spirit. Not only that, multivalent metaphor makes room for *all* the participants to find their place in the ritualized event, so that care and meaning may be conveyed not just to the focal persons, but to everyone.

And fourth, having an overarching metaphor gives structure and meaning to a ritualization. There is a risk when "inventing" a ritual that it will end up being a laundry list of lovely items with no connection or flow—a collection of beautiful ornaments with no tree on which to hang them. Yet a ritual is a single event, as a symphony has four movements but is one musical piece, as a play has five acts but is one dramatic work. While there may be several metaphors and symbols and stories within any rite, it is helpful, particularly in a one-time pastoral rite of passage or healing like Joanie's, to generate a metaphor that enables the planner and the participants to get a sense of the whole and to enable all the pieces to hang together.

A metaphor differs from a *theme* that can be summarized as a fact or discursive statement (for example, "We want to mark an ending to this marriage and establish a new covenant between them"). Broader than a theme, a metaphor's layers of meaning include tone and affect, touching not only the mind but the heart. The whole person is engaged. A foundational metaphor has the power to inspire powerful symbolic action and a deep sense of truth. The metaphor's tone, affect, and action also open the way for artistic expression.

It is important in any Christian ritualization to make apparent the connection between the stories of the focal persons and the story of salvation. In the declaration that begins some wedding services, for example, reference is made to Christ's first miracle at a wedding at Cana, and also to the biblical wedding imagery of the union of Christ with his bride, the church. In funerals one hears the words, "'I am the resurrection and the life,' says the Lord. 'Whoever believes in me, even though they die, yet shall they live.'" In other rites, stories from Scripture are read, so that the worshipers can find their place in the biblical narrative through the connections made in Scripture and sermon. The Scripture read and the imagery used interprets the human situation in light of the story of God's covenant people. As a covenant people, we find our meaning in belonging across history to a people called by God and pledged to loving God and neighbor in holy, ethical living. We cultivate a way of seeing so as to recognize God's loving power at work, bringing all things to fulfillment in the reign of God. Covenanted to God in Christ, we bear the sacred trust of participating in the already-but-not-yet fullness of God's reign, remembering the world to God in prayer[7] and loving the world in self-giving service. Such seeing, such living, is our work—our worship service and our world service.[8] Metaphors help rituals make these connections.

Entering the World of the Metaphor

It is not enough, however, just to *have* a metaphor or perhaps to use it like a decoration, dropping a few related words into a prayer or even draping a half-unraveled cloth over the altar. The power and meaning are unleashed when the (literal) world of the metaphor has been so explored by the focal person with ritual midwives and ritual husbands in advance of the rite that the metaphor becomes embedded in the very operation, words, symbols and action of the ritual. This exploration is called "entering the world of the metaphor" and occurs by means of four categories in the Christian narrative of salvation: creation, sin, judgment, and redemption.[9]

Entering the world of the metaphor is an imaginative exercise, one that engages empathy and play[10] to personify the object, situation, or person whose perspective is being taken. The imaginative leaps generate insights among the group members, bolting them out of staid thought patterns, and sparking openings within which the Holy Spirit can move. In this case, for example, the tablecloth to be unraveled in Joanie's rite could be personified and its "world" entered playfully in terms of creation, sin, judgment, and redemption:

Creation: What is the world like inside this metaphor? (What's it like to be a tablecloth? Give thoughts and feelings.)
Example : My life is happy. I fulfill a purpose. I tie people together. I protect the table, provide beauty, become a homey place for relationships to happen. I am colorful, beautiful, flexible, integrated, fulfilled and fulfilling.

Sin: What goes wrong? (What ruins the tablecloth's world? What upsets or destroys it?)
Example: I'm being unraveled! I'm not used up, but I'm being intentionally undone. I feel helpless! Now I'm nothing but piles of thread—used thread at that—worse than before I was created.

Judgment: What brings this world or the characters in it up short? (What turns my world around? What reverses its direction?)
Example: Well, I'm certainly "dead" as a tablecloth. But it isn't that I'm obliterated. I still exist, just in pieces. Now that I'm unraveled, I could be respun and then woven into something else: another table cloth with a different pattern or a shawl or a vest or a dress. I'm not dead, just disintegrated. I'm hopeful that someone will care enough to reweave all my threads—or some of them—or weave me into several new creations.

Redemption: What brings things around right? (What new life is created? How will the new world look?)
Example: The colors themselves are beautiful, vibrant, interesting. My threads are no longer long enough for weaving. But look! An artist is interested. Free thread! I will be part of an art student's work, a gift to a talented person with few resources. What will it be? I will be the most surprised of all, to find out what I become! Will it be a collage? Part of a painting? Jewelry? I will no longer be on a table. Perhaps I'll be on a wall or around someone's neck. Perhaps I'll be a dream-catcher or become a gift to a loved one. I shall be beautiful again in a way I cannot even imagine!

This gives but a brief example of how this works—yet enough, I hope, to see the power of metaphor to yield symbol that conveys the full complexity of the reality, with all its pain and all its hope. A metaphor can be more completely honest than can discursive speech. And metaphoric honesty contributes to ritual honesty. Certainly, Joanie (who happens to be an artist) will recognize that what is true of the piles of thread is also true of her life: that the remnants of her marriage will be reconfigured in utterly unexpected ways, but ways with beauty and integrity. Others participating in a rite in which this metaphor is used will also be able to draw hope and trust, each in one's own way.

The power for Joanie will come, however, through her drawing the inference herself. The dawning of awareness that her unraveled life will have a new design, at least as beautiful and surprising as her married life, will have power for her largely because she herself will see and know. Her unconscious and conscious, her right brain and left brain, her spirit and her mind, all together will have the possibility of recognizing that what is true for the threads may also be true for her. This dawning awareness cannot emerge in the same way if someone tried to "explain" it to her. It's the inferential conclusion within her that will operate.[11] This is a kind of knowing, akin to faith, made sure and certain by its recognition external to herself. Joanie can recognize it in the threads, unraveled, sitting there, curled up into themselves, but as colorful as ever, waiting. Seeing from the perspective of the threads (the world of the metaphor), her spirit may open to seeing that she, too, still has color, waiting, potential, new life ahead. Someone could say in mere words, "Now, Joanie, your life is not over; it'll just be different. Wait and see. All will be well." These words may be true and they may be comforting. But they will not have the same power as that created by her own hands unraveling the threads, her conversation with friends about what she will do with them, her reflection on her own life while handling them, and the ritual to follow in which the unraveling will be the primary symbol (with other actions and words). (In fact, some years after this ritual, Joanie did make a beautiful creation out of the remnants of the unraveling.) This is the power of metaphor, of beauty, of art.

Seeking an overarching metaphor is important for a pastoral rite. Look to cartoons, to nature, to novels. Look at Scripture, culture, media. Try nursery rhymes, songs, history. It is good to do this exploration with both the focal person and the planning team, because it's whimsical and creative, and because, as with Joanie, sometimes a metaphor has immediate resonance with the focal persons, and then you know that it will have power and meaning for them, that it will operate to work healing within them.

Using metaphor is biblical. Jesus used a series of metaphors to help a variety of people comprehend the reality of the kingdom of God (in Matthew, "kingdom of heaven"). A parable is an extended metaphor in story form that communicates not only insight but startles as a reversal in reality is given. The prophet Ezekiel used enacted metaphor on several occasions. While these were not full rituals, they were strong message bearers for his fellow Jews in exile. To communicate the coming siege of Jerusalem, for example, Ezekiel created an effigy of Jerusalem, and then was told to lie on his left side facing "Jerusalem," one day for every

year of the punishment of Israel (northern tribes): 390 days. Then he
was to move over and lie on his right side, one day for every year of the
punishment of Judah (southern tribes), forty days (Ezek. 4:1-17; see also
5:1-17). While we may hope God never asks us to lie on one side for
over fourteen months, there is no doubt that the physical drama of Ezekiel's prophecy made a lasting impact on his people. This is the power of
symbolic action and enacted metaphor. Well and truly done, it mediates
power, creating redemptive hegemony, though in an unconscious way, as
Catherine Bell points out.

Metaphor creates aesthetic distance. Not only does metaphor penetrate
resistance and communicate the heart of a message; it does so by connecting the particular situation with the wider truth. Working with
metaphor generates an aesthetic distance from the particular individuals
involved in order that the universality of the situation may be seen. Focal
persons can see that they are not alone, because their story is actually a
part of the whole human story of salvation as revealed in Scripture, tradition, reason, and experience.

In addition, *metaphor is the best way to communicate the complexity of life,
including the realities the focal persons are facing.* In every gain, there's a little
loss; in every loss, there's a little gain. Even birthdays celebrate the maturing and "saging" process[12] (as well as the gift of life), while pointing to
realities never again relivable, opportunities not taken—and raw loss.

More importantly, *entering the world of the metaphor reveals the centerpiece of the ritual: its "symbolic action."* Remember that symbols are not
only things or people, but actions. In most (if not all) cases, the focus
of a ritual is a symbolic action. In Joanie's case, the symbolic action will
be the unraveling of the tablecloth. In the case of Patricia, abused by a
clergyman, there were several symbolic actions: washing of feet (current
clergymen washed her feet and apologized on behalf of the church; then
she washed their feet), a journey through the woods, and an anointing.[13]
In another divorce rite, the action was burying the two wedding rings
in the churchyard. In a funeral, it is the burying of the body. In the case
of a woman who had a series of miscarriages, and in her grief became
unable to conceive, the action was walking down to the stream behind
the church and naming each fetus as she set a leaf-boat afloat in the river
(she had carefully made five of them in advance, with friends). In baptism,
it's the washing with water (which is why sprinkling a couple of drops of
water on the baptizand with a rose, for example, misses the significance

intended by the water, since the action is truncated). In communion, it's the eating and drinking of the bread and cup. One could think of sacrament as an *enacted symbol:* a holy symbol *done.*

Finally, *developing a metaphor helps integrate diverse elements into one single event, and extends meaning beyond the rite.* For example, in her later years, my grandmother used a table loom to weave hand towels, tea towels, placemats, and "mug rugs" (coasters). In planning a small service at her retirement community when she died, my weaver friend Judy suggested giving every person a length of yarn and inviting them to weave it into Grandma's unfinished weaving, which Judy would then finish, and give as a memorial art piece for the retirement community. Thus weaving became the overarching metaphor of the memorial service, a symbol of each participant's part in Grandma's life and the reality that our life together "goes on, beautiful,"[14] even though a death has torn a temporary hole in the fabric of community. Judy made it happen through her expertise and leadership, but also as a *servant leader;* for what people remember from that day is less Judy's role than their own creating, the chance to "do something" to honor and remember Grandma. It's tangible love. It's our collective gift for Grandma, but also *with* Grandma, to the next generation of weavers in that community. Even God was honored in this giving.

From Metaphor to Symbol

Because we can trust simple things and actions in creation to signify and mediate God's presence, it makes *sense*—literally—to draw from an apt metaphor a symbolic action in every ritual for healing and passage. Since rituals at times of suffering and transition all seek to effect some level of change in the life and spirit of the focal person, symbolic action is crucial to mediate the sensory ritual power needed. Metaphor makes meaning tangibly and sensorially, and makes it beautiful. When the metaphor is enacted, it can become a symbol. Meaning is made in metaphor, and meaning is stored in symbol.[15]

In relating symbol to metaphor, I draw upon Paul Ricoeur, particularly his lectures collected in *Interpretation Theory.*[16] Ricoeur first shows that metaphor does not just substitute one word or figure for another for the sake of being pleasing or persuasive, as early rhetoricians suggested. Rather, metaphor places two meanings together, which creates a tension of absurdity,[17] only resolved in the awareness of new meaning. One example is "the mantle of sorrow": sorrow is not, in fact, a garment made of cloth. Thus a metaphor does not exist in itself, but "in and through an interpretation" (50)—a conflict of interpretation that generates new meaning. "A metaphor, in short, tells us something new about reality" (53). A real metaphor is thus vibrantly unexpected and ambiguous, it is not found in a dictionary, and it is not translatable (52)—like "sorrow is a mantle" or "this marriage is a tablecloth unraveled."[18] *Metaphors make meaning.*

What distinguishes a symbol from a metaphoric figure of speech, asserts Ricoeur, is that a symbol always refers to something else. It has a referent beyond the point it tries to make in its own context. Metaphor is part of language (for example, "Divorce is an unraveling"). But when the metaphor is enacted, it can become a symbol, and thereby part of reality. Symbols are less words or concepts than *things, people,* and *actions.* The limit of metaphor, says Ricoeur, is the same as the limit of any speech. The wider limit of symbol, by contrast, is the limit of the cosmos (61). Symbol points beyond itself and has a life of its own, a referent beyond its context, which embraces humanity (rather than the other way around).

Universal symbols, as Paul Tillich explains, participate in the very thing to which they point.[19] The moon is more than a metaphor: it is a universal symbol that always represents the feminine, because the pull of the moon affects not only the tides, but the feminine monthly cycle. The earth always represents fecundity because it literally gives life. Light represents seeing (and understanding) because it literally enables one to see. A circle symbolizes (because it creates) oneness; water, cleansing; bread, nourishment.

Symbol, then, stores meaning. Not only that, but symbol is the smallest unit of ritual, notes Victor Turner, the anthropologist whose work is foundational to any study of ritual.[20] Rituals use and are made up of symbols; the centerpiece of any ritual is symbolic action. Without story and symbol, a ritual would not be a ritual. Therefore, any ritual maker needs to know about working with symbols, since symbols are the foundational element of rituals.

Not only is symbol a necessary and powerful vehicle of meaning and action in a ritual, but working well with symbols is essential for ritual competence because good use of symbols leads to "good" ritual—ritual that is true and ethical, and mediates the Holy One while caring for the focal person. By the same token, symbols that are lacking or inadequate or poorly chosen can lead to a ritual backfire.[21] But God is infinite, mysterious, and wonderful. How does one comprehend the intricacy of relationships in one's own family, much less the beauty in all creation? How can a person touch or relate to the wondrous gift of God in Christ? It's too big. Humans cannot apprehend or relate to such grandeur, except through symbol.

For example, I cannot embrace all of God's love in my feeble arms, but I can wear the cross of Christ around my neck. I cannot see the Holy Spirit, but I can adore the Spirit through an icon of Pentecost hanging in my room. I try to feel and utter thanks worthy of the Creator, but I do it best walking in the mountains or on the ocean shore, surrounded by the signs of God's loving beauty. Ritual, as life, relies upon great symbols of the faith and of humanity, including particular symbols meaningful to the focal person, for apprehension of the great truths in which we live. Finding the right symbols and metaphors is a joyous and sacred labor. When working with what gives meaning to persons' lives, the stakes are high, and they are holy. Symbolic competence matters. It is important, therefore, to know where symbols come from, how people can be symbols, and what makes symbols effective and ethical.

From Symbol to Sacrament: The Sacramental Principle

Symbols come to us from creation, from the ordinary stuff of our world. Things and actions used for sacrament are not special things inaccessible to a normal person. To the contrary, what Jesus used for holy actions that connect us with his Abba are common human actions with ordinary elements that come right from creation. The physical world, far from being bad, is the very way through which the beauty and goodness and truth of God is revealed to us. The spiritual is mediated to us through the physical matter of creation. Louis Weil calls this wonder *the sacramental principle.*[22]

"Sacrament" makes "sacred." It does so by setting a symbol (for example, water, bread, wine) into action. A sacrament, then, is a symbolic action, accompanied by scriptural words, done by a designated person, with the intent to do what the church intends by the action. This principle arises out of the incarnation of God in Christ Jesus, a particular human being. If the incarnation teaches us that the particular can mediate the universal—that one man in one time and place can save all people in all times and places—it also teaches us that flesh is the medium of the holy, a means of grace. "Flesh is the hinge of salvation," wrote Tertullian (c. 160–c. 225 CE).[23] God created the physical world; and it is through that very created world that God self-reveals.[24]

This idea can be a scandal to the intellect. In fact, the incarnation and the sacramental principle were rejected by the Docetists who believed that the flesh and the physical were evil, that God was pure spirit and that Jesus (who was flesh) could not, therefore, have been divine. Against Docetism, Jews and Christians believe in treating fleshly bodies and physical things with respect. Creation is holy. Jewish liturgist Lawrence Hoffman notes that when we sit down at the dinner table, the meal before us consists of things that used to be living: holy parts of holy creation. The historic interpretation of table blessing, he writes, is that it removes the lettuce, tomatoes, rice, chicken, tea from its status as creation—desacralizes it, so to speak—so it can become food, so we can unblasphemously eat it.[25] The worldly can mediate the holy, because the world created by the Holy One *is* holy. Symbols of the holy, therefore, come from creation.

The sacramental principle is the truism that the spiritual is mediated or symbolized by created matter, that the ordinary can manifest the extraordinary. Any sense, thing or action may convey meaning and/or spiritual reality. A whiff can bring back a whole relationship and all its meaning, and there you are with your Grandpa, back in the garage as you were every Saturday morning, working on the car together. World War II military chaplain Wayne Rood, who was stationed in the Pacific when the war ended, provides a moving example of the sacramental principle. In the planning conversation for a service of the Lord's Supper, someone suggested the Japanese soldiers nearby be invited. A small group was dispatched to invite them; they accepted. Pastor Rood asked the men what they might use for individual communion cups. One man agreed to provide them. On the morning of the appointed day, here came several hundred cups, enough for everyone—carefully milled out of brass mortar-shell casings. Together, five-year enemies would share the blood of the Lord out of ammunition casings turned into cups of communion. No reference needed to be made to what these were; their proclamation was immediate and real. The men, Allies and Axis the day before, now became brothers as they drank their swords into plowshares, their enmity into communion.[26]

Victor Turner calls *local symbols* like the mortar-casing communion cups, with special meaning in a particular context, "instrumental symbols,"[27] by which he means local or particular symbols effective in a ritual for one particular person(s) but opaque in another. Local symbols can be just as powerful for one family or group as universal symbols are to the whole human family.

Beyond local symbols, then, are *universal symbols* that retain their meaning from one context to the next. Turner calls these "dominant" symbols;[28] Carl Jung calls them "archetypal" symbols. In whatever era or culture you live, or in whatever religion you are a part, the moon, the earth, light, circle, water, bread carry deep human meaning across cultures and religions. The Greek root for symbol (*sym* + *ballein*) is "to throw together." Symbol engenders integrity because of its very participation in, its very creation of, the thing it represents.[29]

In addition to local and universal symbols, there are *Jewish and Christian symbols*, which may or may not overlap with these other categories: for example, the three young men in the fiery furnace in Daniel, the valley of dry bones in Ezekiel, the walls of Jericho tumbling down, the Good Samaritan, the leper who returned to give thanks. Some are archetypal: the exodus, Isaiah's suffering servant. And death and resurrection: Christians understand this central symbolic reality to be an archetype in the whole human family. Christians are at their best proclaiming the truth that God brings life out of death. The death and resurrection of Jesus Christ, the stunning mystery of his passover from death to life, not only points to salvation, but actually effects salvation. The paschal mystery is foundational to every Christian ritual: it is Christian; it is universal; it is central to sacrament; and thus it is central to Christian ritual.

Using Symbols Sacramentally

Symbols are enacted both representationally and literally. Symbols are physical. Tillich's understanding of symbol leads into the sacramental reality, for when symbols are set into action, the result falls in the realm of the sacred, the sacramental. Thus the most powerful symbols are not just objects to be observed, but are actions to be done. The most powerful rituals mirror sacraments in that persons participate in them in both their literal and symbolic meanings.

As powerful as acting symbolically is, many persons who lead worship week by week are unaware of the physicality of symbolic action. For example, one worship team decided on a Sunday theme of "bowing before the Lord." They very carefully integrated words of Scripture, song lyrics, and sermon to include the need to kneel before the Lord, to submit, to bow before the Sovereign King of the Universe. One of my students, serving on the team, finally asked, "So when will we have the congregation actually kneel?" There was confusion and silence. Finally one of the leaders said, "Oh, no, we won't actually *kneel*. We're using this more as a 'symbol.'"

This worship team did not understand what Tillich did, that to be a symbol is to have both figurative and physical components. For the carefully prepared theme of this worship to have actual power, the worshipers had to physically, literally participate in what the symbol pointed to: getting down on the floor on their real, fleshly knees. Maybe it's messy or embarrassing. But once their bodies, their flesh, are in the actual posture of kneeling or bowing down (foreheads on the ground) before the Lord, not only will they never forget that liturgy, but their lives will be changed. Their body memory will live that relationship with God forever. If there's nothing literal or physical about it, then it's not a symbol.

This is true of many Christian actions whether or not they are officially labeled "sacrament." There are certainly archetypal symbolic actions in Holy Baptism (washing with water) and in Holy Communion or the Lord's Supper (eating bread, drinking wine). These actions of washing and eating have an organic meaning already. But in the sacramental context, the reality is accomplished, right there, in the doing of it—as Jesus said, "fulfilled in your hearing" (Luke 4:21).

Other sacramental actions that physically use ordinary things to effect or participate in the very things they signify include anointing with oil and the laying on of hands. Oil, for example, was used after public baths in early cultures to keep the skin from drying out. In the desert, water does not work for cleaning dust and dirt from the tiny crevices in the feet, but oil is perfect. Oil, too, is food, enables the preparation and preservation of food, and is a healing unguent. Anointing with oil was the symbolic action for the making of kings and priests, and is often used in baptism. Physical touch of another human being also symbolizes the very thing it does: it can mediate love, tenderness, care, healing. Laying on of hands can heal by the grace of the Holy Spirit. The primary power in any caring liturgy or healing ritual, whether or not it is officially a sacrament, will come from the physical, literal engagement of ordinary local, universal, or Christian symbols by which the worshipers may encounter the Holy One. The physical mediates the holy. This is the sacramental principle.

People as Symbols

Symbols can be things. They can be people. They can be actions. In worship, the strongest symbols are both things *and* actions—water used to wash—or both people *and* actions—bread that is eaten; kneeling that is enacted; unraveling that is literally, physically done. Every rite should engage at least one such symbol; many rites will engage several.

Planners and leaders of caring and competent Christan liturgies must understand and engage symbolic actions, thing-symbols, and people-symbols toward marking an opening to God's reign. Because people are perhaps least understood as symbols, here are four critical symbolic roles that rite-makers need to recognize and fill.

Honoring the existing symbols: the people. It is often forgotten that people are symbols. One of the major contributions of Vatican Council II was to remind the Western church that there are four primary symbols of the presence of Christ in the Eucharist, the assembly being one.[30] Church architecture began to shift the seating toward curved rows so that the people gathered could see each other, central symbol of Christ. People may be symbols consciously or unconsciously. It is valuable for a ritual planner or leader to recognize and honor the symbolic valence of the people involved, since people often bear the strongest symbolic power. Clergy, police, doctors, judges, and teachers bear symbolic meaning inasmuch as they stand for a profession on behalf of the whole people. Symbol bearing carries a sacred trust and thus calls for an ethical commitment. Betrayal of that trust by symbolic persons is a heinous sin of itself, but additionally because that violation of trust taints every other person bearing that symbolic role and leaves the vulnerable afraid to trust anyone.

The leader is a symbol. In Christian ritual, the leader/pastor, lay or ordained, is a symbol of authority, pastoral care, the *ecclesia*, and to some, of God. Participants put their trust in the leader to guide them through from the beginning of the rite to the end. It is for this reason that persons bearing symbolic power are often well able to act on behalf of others. A leader bears symbolic meaning best when, during the rite, she or he can be a prayerful, Godly presence, and keep focused on the participants and their experience. A good leader exudes trust and confidence[31] so that participants can be at ease without worrying about what they'll be asked to do or what is coming next.

In order to carry this spiritual symbolism, a good leader will have confidence that all the arrangements have been made. The most competent leaders I have witnessed have prepared carefully, by walking through all the steps and imagining every transition, cue, and possible pitfall in advance. That way, during the ritual itself, they can focus on the Holy Spirit's work among the people, and instill confidence and trust. Because nervous participants cannot fully receive the gifts and power of a rite, the best leaders enable participants to let go of anxiety about how the rite is going in order to engage fully in the meaning and power of the ritual action.

A common risk for ritual leaders, especially new ones, is a lack of trust in the ritual structure or in the power of the Holy Spirit to work during a ritual. Without their own inner trust and confidence, leaders may collapse the ritual ethos into overpersonalized familiarity. Some rites are indeed casual and folksy, and that is their strength. But the power of rite, and therefore the reason for ritual in the first place, is that it invites persons into a context that is a strategic contrast with the everyday, so it is *not* business as usual. To lead a rite as if it were the same as a spontaneous meeting of friends may risk being ineffective with vulnerable persons. Focal persons and other participants need the freedom to focus on their own situations and on what God is doing in and for them. If no one seems to be in charge of the rite, the focal persons are likely to have a divided mind, trying to manage it from their observer role as well as participate from their vulnerability, and the power for them will be diminished.

A second risk is that unprepared or insecure leaders may look for a congregational response to affirm their competence or to assure them that their leadership is being well received. In this case, leaders will have divided focus: part of their mind-heart will attend to the participants' needs, but another part will be used up in concern for their own need for validation. Because worship leaders are symbols, they have a responsibility to be translucent so that worshipers can see "through" them to focus on what God is doing and not on the worship leaders themselves. This requires that leaders prepare themselves spiritually in advance, so that they are open to the Spirit, grounded, centered, clear, selfless, trusting, and confident. These two—disciplines praying for spiritual presence, and preparing and rehearsing arrangements—make it possible for the leader

to be unself-conscious and thus a more pure and translucent symbol for
the people.

The focal person is also a symbol. People cry at weddings partly because
they see themselves represented in the bride and groom, remembering
hopes both fulfilled and failed. A man who has lost his wife of fifty-eight
years may find a wedding to be both a time to celebrate and a time to
weep. This is not only normal, it is helpful for a community, because
there aren't that many socially acceptable times when a man can cry for
his beloved wife, now deceased. The bride and groom are symbols for him
and for all the guests. Even in a small ritual like what Joanie was planning, the two witnessing couples there to support and participate will
feel the symbolic valence of hope and brokenness for Frank and Joanie,
and will for days think about their own marriages, what is broken, what
is healing, what holds them together. For that ritual, Joanie and Frank
are symbols.

The participants are also symbols. Christian ritual is done in the church,
by the church, and on its behalf. It is the *ecclesia,* the ones "called out,"
the body of Christ, which mediates caring liturgies for the focal persons.
First, therefore, *worshipers represent the holy church in all times and places.*
Only a few can be present, but because *they* are there, the *church* is there.
The people are the most important symbol in any worship service, equal
with the bread and wine, for worship is an encounter between God in
Christ (symbolized in the word proclaimed and in bread and wine) and
God's people (symbolized in the assembly and the presider). The Holy
Spirit is invoked in many eucharistic services to make the bread and cup
and the people into the body of Christ. Without the people, there is no worship. We worship on each other's behalf, as discussed earlier. Participants
symbolize the church. And they are also witnesses, representing all the
other witnesses who cannot be present (in this world and the next, including saints and angels). The role of witness is essential, for it makes real the
action of the Spirit in the lives of the focal people.

Finally, there may be persons in the rite with special symbolic importance. A
competent ritual planner will listen to the focal person's stories to identify persons who mediate a symbolic role, and make sure these persons
would be invited to take part in the rite. For example, in a rite for a
young person gone astray and trying to turn his life around, inviting the
godfather who was present at his baptism or the pastor before whom he
first professed his faith may symbolize continuity in God's love and call,

and represent a particular kind of care for the young man. Or, at a funeral, the presence of someone who had been alienated from the deceased can be a welcome sign of forgiveness and reconciliation, marking death as a statute of limitation on resentment, and making peace for the deceased as well as for others. Family and friends of the focal person are often meaningful symbols, either in their presence or in their absence.

Effective Symbols: Symbolic Rupture

In addition to the rich symbols people can be, a meaningful rite also shifts people's vision of their life and widens their life context. According to Louis-Marie Chauvet, this occurs by providing the proper amount of what he calls *symbolic rupture.*[32] Chauvet means that for ritual to be effective, it must have a balance of similarity with and difference from ordinary reality. Many ritual leaders never think of this critical need. Here are examples of both ends of the symbolic rupture spectrum.

On the one hand, if a ritual is just business as usual, the same kind of event as an educational experience or a concert, or just like a normal weekday supper, it will lack the power of passage and healing because it will fail to draw the person into "another world to live in."[33] Christian ritual, Chauvet demonstrates, must create a certain rupture from normal quotidian living in order to function.

Chauvet's point is another way of describing what the Bible calls "holiness," which in Hebrew means "set apart" from the ordinary. The Sabbath day is different from the other days: distinguished, defined in a different category, treated especially. The outward sign of this setting apart is the different treatment given to the day, the people, and the animals on this day of rest and reverence. When the children of Israel were in exile in Babylon, their very identity was established through keeping holy the Sabbath in this countercultural way. It was often difficult, invoking disparagement and even ridicule. It did set them apart from the local culture as those who serve the Lord. Chauvet exaggerates this a bit, calling the difference a "rupture" from the ordinary. But the importance of the need for this symbolic rupture cannot be exaggerated.

If there is no aesthetic and spiritual distance from the everyday, no "other," then there is no power to critique the quotidian. A religion's ritual is its public identifying mark as well as an entrée into and an instance of another world. The very contrast between the holy world of the ritual and the ordinary (= profane) world of the daily enables worshipers to see and grasp the holy living they're supposed to do, the baptismal life they've committed to.

On the other hand, if the symbolic rupture is too much, if there is little relationship between what occurs in the ritual and what everyday life is like, then the ritual is merely foreign and lacks the power to affect the everyday. There must be enough continuity between the ritual and ordinary life to show a path by which participants may step from the ordinary world into the holy religious world.

Worshipers must be able to recognize themselves in the ritual action, which must be relevant to the participants' lives, and related to what they face daily. For example, Joanie came up with a metaphor from her world of fabric art, and also from her lifelong eucharistic experience of table symbolism. For another person, the defining metaphor with the right balance of continuity and rupture might be planting a tree.

In hermeneutic language, in order to comprehend anything, you have to have a "preunderstanding"—an interpretive framework shaped by prior experience—by which to imagine what might be at play. It takes an interpretive lens through which to comprehend an invitation to let go of normal noise and enter into sacred silence, into the Holy One. It is challenging work to proffer an experience that draws people beyond the ordinary in such a way that they can infer holiness themselves from the very experience, without drawing them so far beyond the familiar that they are unable or too frightened to accept the invitation. Creating just the right amount of symbolic rupture, however, is the challenging art of the ritual leader: the rupture must not be too small or there will not be enough difference to make meaning; but it also must not be too great or the participants will not be able to understand it or relate to the rite. Ritual action must strike a balance between inviting participants into an "other" world, mysterious, where the rules and expectations may be different, and the "daily" world where they live in repetitive cultural patterns. The "other" world gives a wider vision, even a cosmic perspective, but the purpose of this vision is to enable persons to operate differently in their daily world. The coming together of two worlds in a ritual container that offers a strategic contrast with the ordinary is what enables persons to find the holy in the earthly and to live an ordinary life that is divine.

Using Symbols Ethically

Ritual makers, then, will use universal symbols, symbols of the faith, and local symbols particularly meaningful to the focal person in developing a ritual. But it is also possible to use symbol and metaphor shallowly or carelessly, and therefore *unethically,* and this must always be avoided.

"Symbol gives rise to thought,"[34] according to Ricoeur. Symbol and metaphor are not just "nice comparisons." They are also philosophical categories. They are used in theological and moral reasoning. They teach; they inform; they empower. The intellectual and/or visceral understanding produced by an apt metaphor or a powerful symbol informs the mind and the heart. Metaphors and symbols can change people's opinions, their understanding, even their motivations. Thought is part of meaning. Symbols, thoughts, and meanings are dangerous. They can be life giving and transformative. They can be deadening and isolating. The power and importance of the use of strong symbols in any worship, including rites of passage and healing, is central to the making of meaning in twenty-first-century post-Christendom, and is critical as worship and its theologies emerge into a new millennium, a new paradigm.

Philosopher Susanne K. Langer has identified "symbolization" as the current generative idea, which is how meaning is made.[35] Through symbolization, we are able to study "the *human response,* as a constructive, not a passive thing,"[36] resulting in such current studies as agency,[37] lay ministry, psychology,[38] and other fields of human empowerment. Symbolization opens a door into "the essentially *transformational* nature of human understanding."[39] Symbol gives rise to thought. Symbol transforms.

If Langer is right, the exploration of symbol and its effect on meaning and transforming human personhood has barely begun. Her subtitle is *A Study in the Symbolism of Reason, Rite, and Art.* I see the tremendous interest in and creation of art in worship as part of what Langer calls "symbolic transformation."[40] Langer, a student of Alfred North Whitehead, identifies an interpretive framework that helps us, for example, to comprehend the dissatisfaction many feel with traditional worship forms and the longing for engaged creativity in worship. If the postmodern inkling is correct that truth and meaning are no longer most fully mediated through linear rationality, then how are they to be perceived? According to Tillich, Langer, Ricoeur, and others, it is through symbol and symbolic transformation. As important to the evolution of human thought as modern thought forms are, linear rational discourse is inadequate when trying to know or relate to God. As Tillich said, that which for humans is of "ultimate concern must be expressed symbolically, because symbolic language alone is able to express the ultimate"—that is, God.[41] Therefore, trying to generate vibrant, passionate worship without seeing how symbol operates, risks making another version of empty form, devoid of the meaning for which people are starving today.

Meaning is made in metaphor and is stored in symbol. Making apt metaphors and using symbols carefully, in the service of life and truth as revealed in Christ, can carry persons from one "world" to another or restore them to the world of their baptized life in Christ on a journey into God. This can best be done if not only the metaphors and symbols, but all the elements of the ritual, are honest. This is the next method for creating caring liturgies, and the next principle: making honest ritual that mediates the whole truth.

4

Ritual Honesty
Holding Truthful Tension

🕊 Ritual making is a serious enterprise. Because rituals are so powerful, a cavalier approach can fail to accomplish the rite's life-giving goal, exacerbate difficulties, or even cause harm. Christian ritual is a rope intertwined with four cords: pastoral, theological, ecclesial, and ethical. What is so artful about ritual is that all these are integrated into a single action. To assure their strength and balance, however, the rope must be sheathed in ritual honesty.[1] The principle offered in this chapter, assuring the honesty of any Christian rite, begins with ethics; for good pastoring is always ethical and all theology should be ethical. Yet implications for the other three strands, pastoral, theological, and ecclesial, will be made clear in stories throughout the chapter. Joanie's story will lead us into five aspects of ritual honesty.

Five Aspects of Ritual Honesty

Every ritual involves giving and receiving, the interaction utterly central to the Christian life. God gives; God first loved us. All is gift. It is inasmuch as we receive that we are able to recognize the gift, and offer back what little we have: our tithe, our thanks. Sometimes deep giving, pouring oneself out for another, can be a true labor of love. It is important not only for the focal persons to spend themselves before the rite, but it can be important for the support persons and witnesses to do the same.

I was delighted to discuss with Grace contributions she and the other witnesses might make to the ritual and thus to Joanie and Frank, to support them each and both in this tenuous and tensive time. Grace planned to offer her art form and write a poem. It made me glad, for it would be personal, beautiful, and true, as well as a labor of love, a deep gift for our friend. But then my delight shifted suddenly to distress when Grace announced, "Barbara has offered to bring the main dish for a meal afterward." My heart missed a beat as an uneasy "No!" arose from my spirit. My own reaction startled me, for every liturgy, every worship service, every ritual I'd ever been a part of had centered around food or had ended with a shared meal. And it was right and good for Barbara to make her offering of love and care for Frank and Joanie. But I knew that in this case, trying to share a meal would be a terrible mistake. What was wrong?

It is standard practice in both Christian and other faith traditions to follow worship with a meal. All humans eat; eating (of special foods, in special ways, at special times) underlies the religious and ritual practices of all humanity. What is there at the end of a Bar/Bat Mitzvah, at sundown during Ramadan, after a wedding or Shabbat service or a Lord's Day service? At the end of an ordination, a baptism, even a funeral? There is a feast, a repast, a reception. There is hospitality and graciousness, formal trays of carefully made hors d'oeuvres, vases of flowers, color-coordinated napkins. There is casual comfortability, a warm "help yourself" welcome. There is hot coffee, iced punch, bottles of something. There are aromas to tempt the tongue, colorful patterns to delight the eye. There is plenty. There is, in short, a celebration involving food.

So it was natural for one of Joanie's supporters to begin to plan the meal after the ritualization. This was the death of a marriage. Every honoring of death she had ever known needed someone (who was not the focal person) to coordinate the food—and so she offered.

But on this occasion, sharing food would not have been appropriate. It wouldn't have worked. No one could have eaten. To try to share a meal would have conflicted utterly with what had just been done in the ritual. How could they have broken bread together after they had unraveled the dining tablecloth, separated the furniture, and parted company? Eating together is a sign of unity: one board, one loaf, sharing one meal. But the point of this ritual was that there was no longer a shared table, a common cloth, a united marriage. Trying to eat together that day would have broken the symbol and confused the meaning. It would have enacted forced unity when in fact separation and disunity had just been honestly proclaimed. Trying to eat together on that day would have placed everyone in an untenable, awkward situation. (What would they have talked about?) Eating together is normal daily fare—but a broken marriage is utterly unnormal, undaily, sad, and tragic (even if sometimes also lifegiving and necessary). To try to eat together that day would have been dishonest.

1. A Ritual Sets a Dominant Feeling-Tone

When the dominant feeling-tone of a ritual is compromised or when a dominant tone is selected that is not ultimately life giving, the ritual is dishonest. For example, Sunday celebrates the day of resurrection, and so always bears joy and gladness—sometimes unmitigated, sometimes muted. Toward the *celebration* end of the continuum, Sunday worship is inherently felicitous and full of praise, thanks, and rejoicing—that is its basic feeling-tone. Therefore, to make Sunday worship ultimately gloomy with no good news is to violate the centerpiece of the Christian faith: life eternal in God through Christ's resurrection on the first day of the week. Even during Lent or even if a tragedy has occurred during the week and the congregational tone is sober, the inherent meaning of Sunday worship is still Christ's resurrection, and thus leans toward celebration.

By contrast, Good Friday is the day of the crucifixion, a day of pain and agony, denial and betrayal. Of course, this is part of the process of redemption, a necessary step without which there could be no resurrection. However, the tonal range of Good Friday leans toward lament and penitence. And this can be a gift for worshipers. To invite persons into the feeling-tone of the day in which Jesus' suffering is made real can enable worshipers to acknowledge their own suffering, betrayal, pain, and agony. The honest connection with sin and death in Good Friday worship can be liberating and highly experientially effective because of this integrity. To dispense with the anguish of the cross too quickly would change the dominant feeling-tone of Good Friday and close off the possibility of persons connecting their own honest suffering with that of Jesus.

It is important for a ritual leader to discern an appropriate affective and spiritual feeling-tone, a movement that is true both theologically and experientially. This is the first aspect of ritual honesty.

In any change there is always a loss, and always a gain. This is part of the challenge of identifying an affective movement for a ritual action. If both are present, which should predominate? In the case of Joanie and Frank, marking the unraveling of their marriage was honest; the covenant "til death us do part" was broken. Yet here, too, was a new beginning for Joanie's individuation as person and for Frank's career. Is this more lament or more joy?

We will see in the next section that multiple affections are juxtaposed in any ritual: loss next to gain, praise next to lament. Yet before the joy of new beginnings comes the lament of brokenness. This ritual fittingly unravels the marriage. For Joanie and Frank, the dominant tone, expressed by the enacted symbol, was lament for the unraveling of their communion.

Loss can be difficult to ritualize, as noted above, because fear of loss strikes close to home for witnesses and rite-makers. I have seen persons lose their jobs, their pregnancy, their house, their business, their reputation, their health—and their "friends," like Job's friends, are inclined to treat them as if they have done something wrong, as if they are at fault, separating from them as if their losses were contagious. Yet rites of lament, like Joanie and Frank's, can help persons weep over and accept the changes they did not choose, which is the one essential for moving through to new life. In rites of loss and lament, unwanted feelings can be safely expressed, such as anger or self-deprecation or unnameable feelings similar to guilt or shame. Scripture selected may include shaking the dust off one's sandals (Mark 6:11; Luke 9:5), the Exodus story, or the rich young ruler (Mark 10:17-29; Luke 18:18-29). Such rites can keep the sense of loss from devolving into self-loathing or resentment, both in the focal person as well as in others who may be experiencing unidentified shame due to the focal person's pain. The gospel story can contextualize the focal person's feelings. Hope can come from the promise of walking, even in loss, into the future God is already preparing.

On the other hand, if the focal person really was involved in an ethical infraction or injustice, the tonal movement would be oriented toward lament, confession, and reconciliation. Proclaiming forgiveness would be absolutely essential in such a rite; but if it comes too soon, it could be experienced as "cheap grace" and fail to restore the person to full personhood in Christ. Thus any ritual action would be postponed until these issues are sorted out. A different kind of pastoral spiritual care would first be needed: the focal person would be helped through a process of repentance and amendment of life.

First, he or she identifies one's own responsibility as the cause or source of alienation from self, others, and/or God, similar to step four in a twelve-step program. Second, similar to step five, one names (confesses) one's responsibility and participation. A ritual setting is often most comfortable for this. Pastors and spiritual guides are commonly ones to hear such confession. Naming before a witness is difficult, but absolutely necessary for healing to occur within the focal person. Third, one corrects the action and makes amends to those who have been harmed. This could be accomplished before the rite but symbolized during the rite. And fourth is the pronouncement or assurance by "another human being" of God's forgiveness in Christ.

The ritual process may involve several months of working with confession and repentance in sorrow and humility, then moving toward planning and participating in a ritual manifesting lament and repentance, forgiveness and relief, gratitude and new ministry.

The first aspect of ritual honesty, then, is to draw not only on the person's feeling-state, but also on the theology of Christian faith, in order to identify an appropriate dominant feeling-tone for the ritual. Ritual honesty calls for the spiritual, affective experience of the focal persons to be juxtaposed with the spiritual, theological truths of the faith in a way that honors their experience and gives life through Christ in the Spirit. Thereby one can create a ritual in which the focal person can find healing or passage grounded in the grace of God.

2. Accommodating a Wide Range of Feelings and Thoughts

Having assessed the most honest dominant tone for a ritual, the second aspect of ritual honesty may seem contradictory: intentionally making room for a wide range of appropriate emotions, dispositions, and affects. Ritual is valuable in healing and passage or transformation because it is a genre—a container—big enough to hold complex realities together in one moment, one event. I imagine ritual operating along a tonal, affective continuum, marked by celebration at one end, and lament at the other. While holding focus on the dominant feeling-tone, it is also important for ritual planners and leaders to claim the length of the tonal keyboard, black notes as well as the white, and learn to play all the chords in major as well as in minor keys. Some rituals may span most of the notes, in higher drama and greater length. There may even be several movements in a single ritual. Other rituals may focus on a more narrow range, lingering down in lament or trilling in joy, tendering romance or tapping in sharp staccato. All the possibilities from joy to lament are there, but most of us, used to a narrow familiar middle range, shy away from playing notes in the extreme, even if they truly bear upon the situation.

Ritual leaders need to be attentive to a wide affective range, not least because focal persons are often experiencing something extreme that falls outside the average acceptable range, and they don't know what to do with it. In some cultures, for example, it is considered extreme to express outrage, or righteous anger, or to sob loudly. When people have meta-feelings of guilt or shame at experiencing such intense thoughts and feelings, they may try to suppress or deny them. If a ritual planner/ leader plays only in the middle, major keys, then the focal person who is down three octaves is at risk of feeling more odd and "out of it" after the rite than before. Ritual composers need to hold a wider range in mind. First, being daring, they need to enter fully, deeply, into the truth of the spiritual feeling-tone of the focal person, even if it should be at the extreme end of lament or the extreme end of joy. They must not shy away from playing the truth. And second, being wise, they need to compose the modulation of joy into sorrow and lament into hope. They must remember that lament and rejoicing are two sides of one coin and that the human psyche holds together sets of competing and contradictory feelings, meanings, and understandings.[2] Both major and minor chords must be used in any effective and honest ritual.

For example, though the joy of resurrection predominates in Sunday worship, the Sunday after a national emergency will not have the same tone as Easter Day. It would be ritually dishonest to try to cause people to be only joyous when people's hearts are heavy. The spiritual hospitality offered by our Lord makes space in the living room of his heart for the truth of all our feelings and experiences, that they may be welcomed and there find healing and transformation. There is nothing more false than the pretend happiness imposed on a people expected to clap when they can't remember their reason for living. Without the minor theme, it is not a concerto. Honest celebration always has room for those who cannot or do not celebrate that day, and honest lament always remembers the hope attested to by God's salvific intervention throughout history, even in direst times.

On the one hand, then, a ritual has a primary foundational affective and spiritual feeling-tone, theologically understood. And on the other hand, it also makes room to include a contrasting tone or perhaps a multiplicity of contradictory meanings. Like the weeds and the wheat (Matt.

13:28-30), they need to be allowed to coexist. This necessary minor theme is what enables people to laugh at funerals and cry at weddings. The story of Vivian illustrates how openness to a wide range of notes is essential for the music of ritual honesty.

Three days after Vicki made contact with her, Vivian confessed to her congregational women's group that she had become pregnant while in college, given birth, and put her baby up for adoption. After thirty years of longing for a chance to reconnect with her long-lost child, her daughter had called and expressed a desire to meet her birth mother. In tears, Vivian shared her plans to travel to meet Vicki, and the group prayed with her and rejoiced in the possibility of this reunion of mother and daughter. One member, Julia, later pondered how the group might be more supportive, possibly in some ritual way, and thought of hosting a sort of baby shower as a send-off for Vivian's trip. However, the more Julia contemplated the idea, she realized that it certainly could not be a surprise gathering, and that Vivian undoubtedly had even more complex feelings about this situation than she had already shared, which needed careful handling. Rather than risk violating Vivian's spiritual process, Julia decided to invite her to lunch, so she could express the group's desire to send her off in an honest celebration with signs of their love, and to ask what Vivian might like.

Julia was appropriately sensitive to the reality that as blessedly joyous as the "gain" was for Vivian in finding her daughter, the "loss" was very real and present. While there was no denying that celebration would predominate at the ritual, the gain-loss together were a holy and tensive truth for Vivian, one anyone planning or leading a ritual must understand and respect.

For some women in Vivian's situation, however, celebration might not be the dominant affect. It might be shame or guilt or anger. A ritual for such a woman would not at first be a celebration, but might be a lament or a confession, perhaps followed by thanksgiving and letting go. Psychological work might be needed first, before a ritual, and perhaps afterwards as well. Attentiveness to the honest situation of the focal person, as well as to the range of feelings honestly present, is the work of the competent ritual leader. Time and care must be taken.

To be able to hear the focal person's heart accurately, it is helpful for the ritual maker herself to engage the full range of human experience from joy to lament. Both are part of the human experience. Both are expressed in Scripture. All are created and redeemed by God. There is nothing too far out to be heard, accepted, addressed, and lifted before the Lord.

Some rituals operate at the joy end of the spectrum. At the far end of joy might be Christmas and many weddings. And at the tip is Easter Day, when all the stops are pulled out and the music is as if from angels. People come dressed in their finest, bringing their relatives and other guests, and the church house is filled with flowers and trees and color and swooping banners. Neighbors and strangers appear in eager anticipation, and the hinge point of the year is gloriously manifest in undaunted extravagance.

On the far end of the lament tone are rituals for occasions when both human and divine spirits have been violated. Ultimate injustice, degradation, unfreedom, hatred, falsehood and dishonor challenge the very possibility of living in relationship with self or God or one another. These are cases in which ritual action is most needed, yet these rituals are among the most challenging to prepare, such as when a community is touched by senseless violence. In such cases, lament is a normal human affective response.

Perhaps the best expression of lament is found in the Bible, especially in the Psalms. For example, Psalm 137 is a lament, reflecting the experience of people who were ripped from their homes and force-marched to Babylon, where the foods, the language, the religion, the culture were utterly foreign. Its final verse (v. 9), aimed at Babylon, is especially difficult: "Happy shall they be who take your little ones and dash them against the rock!" Many versions of the psalter omit that verse altogether, and few sermons are preached from this text. However, when these verses are taken as lament, as anguished outcry by a violated and victimized people, this ceases to be interpreted as a scandal in the biblical canon. Instead, it becomes not a call to action but a normal, nonrational outrage fantasy. Anyone who has had to witness an act of intentional violence to a loved one will be forgiven for *feeling like* doing the same to the perpetrator's children.[3]

Many, by the grace of God, have never experienced "the hour of lead," as Emily Dickinson called it.[4] But many have known such inhuman trauma that their sense of "normal" has been violated to the core. After appropriate psychological work, such feelings are exactly what can be healed or transformed in the ritual process. Forgiveness takes time, and comes with healing. Some wounds, those that cut down to the inner flesh, must heal from the inside out. If the skin closes over too quickly, infection will set in, and not only does the wound itself not heal, but the whole organism is at risk of death. To live requires keeping the wound open long enough for it to heal at the deepest inside place, and work its way out. The healing process, therefore, is extremely painful.

For some agonies, expressing lament with all its feelings can be the first step in healing: the core outcry from an unspeakable pain. And the feelings of lament are legion: anger, rage, self-deprecation, immobilization, apathy, self-absorption, shame, guilt, taintedness, flatness. Typically such extreme emotions are well worked with before a rite, in pastoral care or counseling, in anger work, in retreat and spiritual guidance, with deep nurture, and the rite would come later. This is what happened to Joanie. In other cases, a rite needs to enable the person to begin the very throes of such pathos, and bring it into the context of the sweep of salvation and into contact with God's tender lovingkindness. As Don Saliers puts it, worship is always a moment when human *pathos* is brought into juxtaposition with divine *ethos*.[5]

Sometimes the true name of the pathos cannot be found. A good ritual, however, can allow the feelings to exist, and often to be healed, even without being named. Thus ritual honesty requires the leader/planner to identify and evince the dominant feeling-tone or melodic line inherent in the ritual event, and then the secondary feeling-tone, while also including harmonies and disharmonies with all the consonant and dissonant overtones, without denying or avoiding chords that seem contradictory. When this happens, a healing juxtaposition is created between theology or belief (that is, "Nothing can separate us from the love of God who has covenanted us with each other and Godself") and the precipitating affect or feeling (such as "I want to kill someone, to die, to give up, to explode in rage"). Through the ritual, participants may find themselves singing in a new key (for example, "In this solidarity, I find my first energies turning into hope and a desire to build something new, good, healing, redemptive"). This juxtaposition of hope and lament is central to Christian theology, Christian worship, and Christian daily living. Gordon Lathrop refers to it as a "juxtaposition of contraries," which God creates and redeems, always "for the sake of life":

> The Christian liturgy . . . embraces contraries: life and death, thanksgiving and beseeching, this community and the wide world, the order expressed here and the disorder and chaos we call by name, the strength of these signs and the insignificance of ritual, one text next to another text that is in a very different voice. . . . The mystery of God is the mystery of life conjoined with death for the sake of life. The name of this mystery revealed among us is Jesus Christ. The contraries of the liturgy are for the sake of speaking that mystery. It is by the presence of these contraries in the juxtapositions of the *ordo* that Christians avoid the false alternatives so easily proposed to us today.[6]

Holding contraries together is more difficult than it may seem. Because North American dominant culture is inclined to hold the expression of emotion to a reasoned mean, a contained balance, a "no big deal" moderate middle, the import of ritual honesty might be missed. Sometimes, the dominant affect of a rite is at the extreme: extreme joy or extreme lament. And when this is the case, the planner/leaders must carefully, courageously enable the *truth of the extreme to be evinced within the safe container of the ritual.* For example, does the death-cracking beauty of worship on Easter day express the zenith of hope and gladness? Is lavishly abundant joy demonstrated in new artistic creations just for Easter, in the clothes of the participants, the glorious music, the participation of the people, the extravagance of procession? And on the other end of the continuum, does worship after the devastation of a natural disaster, or an act of violence, or every Good Friday liturgy, manifest the honest anguish of utter tragedy and loss through ritual wailing, woe-filled silence, words and music of dread and sorrow? An honest ritual allows the fullness of the dominant experience and tone to be expressed, without suppressing the minor secondary tones. In services of celebration, loss is always present; and in liturgies of lament, hope is always manifest. But jumping to hope too soon, or glossing over the lament, renders a ritual dishonest.

One of the wonderful things about ritual is that, like a powerful symbol or a poetic word or a piece of artwork or Scripture itself, ritual can hold the paradox of opposites together without homogenizing them or choosing between them. Participants in ritual can relax into an event that honestly reflects life's complexity and our response to it. There is no need to pretend in an honest ritual or to cut off part of oneself or cover over a few aspects of last week or deny or suppress large chunks of our feelings or our questions or our doubts. There is no need to leave half of ourselves (which doesn't seem to fit the agenda) at the door. There's room not only for each of us, but for *all* of each of us.

The ritual action must be emotionally honest. It must allow the range of feelings persons bring to worship and to hold a truthful tension. Vivian was blessed to have someone with Julia's ritual fluency and competence to comprehend that although she was thrilled to meet her daughter and to celebrate with her friends, it would be emotionally and ritually dishonest to lean toward a celebration that ignored those thirty lost years and denied periodic interjections of guilt and grief. Vivian was in the hands of someone she could trust to make a ritual great enough to hold the whole truth together at once. Therefore, she could relax and focus on receiving the ritual gift: freedom to express and have witnesses to her lament, loss, guilt, gratitude, joy, and future; to tend the family relationships; and to make whatever spiritual turns she needed to make to be utterly healed and free in face of the gift of Vicki in her life.

Every day Vivian has to choose within her emotional self: Where shall I place my focus? In the shadow of the tomb, the guilt and pain and loss thirty years ago and every day in between? Or in the light of the resurrection, giving thanks for my daughter, well raised, now in my life for me to love? Both are true. Sometimes she is tempted toward the tomb. But by the grace of God, almost every day she turns toward the resurrection. To pretend that there is only resurrection and not a real death is to ignore the wounds on Jesus' hands and feet, to deny the truth, to lessen the power of God's work of redemption, and to attenuate, dilute, or "shallowize" the honest daily experience of Vivian's life.

It seems to be human nature to seek stasis, the familiar, even if the balancing act and exertion to hold on means ignoring the evidence or subtle suggestion that the picture is larger than we can see. Faith involves trusting the bigger picture beyond our reach, the picture that includes death, but also resurrection. Our faith gives us a worldview based on the paschal mystery: that there is real death and that this death in Christ is the very seed of life.

Competent ritual avoids an easy stasis, and enables manifestation of truthful tension. Climbing down to the pit of pain and risk is the only way to climb up the other side. Death always, in the fullness of time, gives way to resurrection. This is the Christian hope.

3. Ritual Symbols Must Be True

Having acknowledged the ethical obligation for ritual to be emotionally honest, first through honoring a dominant feeling-tone and second through juxtaposing a secondary tone and perhaps several (even contradictory) beliefs and emotions, we turn to the related third aspect of ritual honesty: that through the tone, words, symbols, actions, persons, and music, rituals *enact what is real*. Ritual does not point to a reality, but it enacts a reality. Its symbols are not tokens or decorations, but loci of value and power.[7] Rituals are where something happens. Something changes. No one leaves a ritual action the same. Rituals are real.

Ritual honesty is an extension of the principle that Christian ritualization engages the paschal mystery in the deaths and resurrections of our daily lives. And resurrection only comes after death. Beginnings only come after endings (and the liminal or neutral zone in between). Without real death, the "life" afterwards holds little meaning. Symbols must be true. That is, symbols must actually signify something. If there is no reality, there is nothing to signify, and any attempt to do so is false. Exchanging wedding vows and rings before the ceremony not only renders the ceremony meaningless, but it turns the exchange of rings into a private devotion with no witnesses to the public reality of a new family created in our midst. Symbols and rituals are real. They change reality; they effect reality. Ritual honesty requires honoring their truth and power.

It is for this reason that work needs to be done before the rite. Psychological or spiritual changes needed must be established before the rite so that the ritual can effect the passage. It is the ritual that creates the change. The focal persons' status is different at the end of a rite of passage than at the beginning. And if the persons are not ready to pass over, the rite will be false; worse, they will be stuck in a pretend world. They were not ready for the changed way of being, but now, having participated in a ritualization, they may feel they should be. It is easy to be caught in immobilization between what one's inner state is (stuck in the past) and what one's public persona is (passed to a new stage). When a graduation ceremony is held before the final papers are submitted, the rite is false, and energy to complete the work can be sapped. When a wedding occurs before the commitment has actually been made on the part of the people, divorce usually follows soon after. When a Quinceañera is given for a young woman marking maturity on her fifteenth birthday, but in fact she is neither mature nor responsible, the new freedoms granted to her can result in disaster. The power of a ritual occurs when it completes and makes real a reality that has already been in the making, for which there is preparation and readiness.

For a ritual to be honest, a temperature must be taken of the honest situation of the focal person. It is critically important not to allow something untrue to be signified. Thus conducting rituals too soon can create a dishonest ritual.

Joanie and Frank's ritual was not too soon. It was conducted at the very end, long after there was any hope of the marriage's self-correction. Vivian had worked through to acceptance over the years. She wisely gave herself a month to prepare for her visit to Vicki. Julia's ritual for her would be planned carefully with no hurry; it would serve as an emotional-spiritual bridge to the public acknowledgment of this reality. A nineti-eth birthday celebration might not be conducted on the exact day of the birthday, but it would not be done in the eighty-eighth year, either, for that would seem more a spoof than an authentic celebration.

4. Ritual Involves Everyone Present

A fourth aspect of ritual honesty is the importance of not forgetting that everybody in the ritual will be affected by it: not just the focal person, but all the participants. While the focus is on the person seeking healing or passage, all the persons present are worshiping, all the persons are car-ing, all are listening, all are witnessing, and all will come away changed by the experience.

Like the performative arts of drama, ballet, or symphonies, ritual exists only while it's happening, in its enactment. The score or playscript or ritual words are guides to the event, but they are not the event them-selves. Yet in spite of this similarity, ritual differs from all of these perfor-mative art forms because in ritual, *all are performers*. There is no audience. In this way, ritual action is less like a drama and more like a conversation in which all are participants, though the style and strength of participa-tion may vary. Ritual is a group experience.

While storytellers are compared to sinners of cotton or wool, recounting an ever-lengthening "yarn," a conversation may be compared to a weaving in which a thread, wound through various designs, can be followed through the whole tapestry. The conversationalists are group contributors to the story. There is a covenant of honesty and trust. Con-versationalists pay rapt attention to the subject and to each other's contri-butions, for all share responsibility for the golden thread woven through the whole. One person shares an insight or piece of information. Another connects that insight to his own experience, personalizing the content, increasing intimacy in the group, and enfleshing the insight. Someone else picks up the thread and weaves it into a book she is reading. Several then comment on the book, a subconversation that goes on for several minutes. Then the thoughtful, quiet one in the corner elegantly twists several ideas together, so that the original thread is reintroduced in a now strengthened floss with more meaning than before. The result is unique;

it belongs to those who were there, who created it together. It is not a "product." It is not visible. But it exists with force, and it may be remembered forever. When the conversation has integrity, everyone is uplifted.

If each person focuses on the shared topic, contributing from experience, then there is trust that each one can also work on one's own connections and insights. However, if one person dominates, the flow is stopped, corporately as well as individually. If there is a leader or host, the job is not to control the conversation, for that ruins it, but to attend to the structure: inviting a quiet person to speak by asking an earnest and related question, for example, or deflecting a dominator, or serving refreshments to renew the spirit when there is a lapse in the energy. A good conversation makes room for all its participants.

Like a conversation, a ritual has a leader who attends to the structure (sequence, timing) but does not control the activity as one would control a computer program or a power plant. Like a conversation, some speak with fluency, some hardly speak at all, yet all levels of participation are honored. Like a conversation, a ritual has a primary thread that participants have covenanted to knit, relate to, and unwind, while individual connections and insights are constantly clicking. Like a conversation, ritual action is a covenanted activity. The ritual is successful inasmuch as everyone enters the covenant, which is sometimes explained for newcomers. Like a conversation, certain manners or etiquette serve as shorthand guides for keeping the covenant (Don't talk when someone else is talking. If you can, stand to sing, sit to listen. Honor God in posture, silence, speech.) Like a conversation, there is a deeper ethic: don't cause people to reveal more than they wish to reveal, don't violate confidentiality, hold everyone's freedom intact, be sensitive to everyone's vulnerability, keep the covenant of not dominating or stopping the flow. Be honest. And like a conversation, each participant in a ritual will come away with something personally, uniquely for him or her, even though it has been a communal event, centered on the focal persons, and always on the Holy One who is greater than all of us put together.

Thus, like a good conversation, at the end people feel refreshed and satisfied, for they have participated in something greater than themselves, something uplifting, something true and honest. Honesty is essential for any good conversation and any good ritual. If untruth is spoken, if people put on airs, then the event is fake, a waste of time, and can sometimes even negate the spirit of celebration it was intended to honor.

5. Allowing the Creative Tension of Opposites to Abide Together

Related to the importance of openness to a wide range of affective themes in a ritual and assurance that everyone will be invited to participate is the fifth aspect of ritual honesty: allowing the inherent tensions to live without resolving them. The tension of two perspectives is aptly illustrated in the story of Rick and Maureen.

Rick was sick of his job, but felt that he couldn't quit because he felt an overwhelming responsibility to provide for his family. While he usually didn't complain, he sometimes managed to relax and talk about his dreams, which entailed a very different life from the one he was living. His wife, Maureen, worried for Rick, since he was so obviously miserable and increasingly distant, but all her efforts to encourage him to quit and follow his dreams met with resistance and sometimes fights. When the day came that Rick found himself laid off from his job, Maureen broke out in spontaneous jubilation, thinking this was a blessing, opening up the possibilities he was avoiding. But Rick, already frantic about how he would meet his family obligations, exploded over her apparently crazy behavior. Maureen didn't seem to understand the direness of their situation, and Rick felt overwhelmed by rage, loss, and now loneliness.

What Scripture would you choose for a job-end ritualization for Rick and Maureen? How would you honor the honest risk, Rick's fear, and the huge unknowns, on the one hand, and yet allow the possibilities and promise to be present on the other?

In preparation for this ritual, it would be very important for the leader to acknowledge the tension between Rick and Maureen, and far from avoiding it, to help them work with it, through the developing of a metaphor. The tension is difficult, but true. It is creative. There is a gift in it that may be found if, instead of denying or disparaging it, the couple can be guided to enter into the tension with gentleness. For example, the leader might help this couple with a process of naming each one's thoughts and feelings, and helping each to generate a vibrant metaphor expressing the opposites and contradictions. Here is where a metaphor is exceptionally helpful, for metaphors hold tensions. If they can work with metaphor, they will be able to enter into the tensive middle ground just off shore where the tide seems to be both coming in and going out at the same time.

But this is *tensive*. Entertaining both his anger and her joy at the same event creates tension. In a highly stress-filled culture, many approaches to eliminating tension have been created, including laughing, minimizing, and deflecting. For a ritual to mediate any power to heal or transform disparity and honest conflict, however, the ritual leader must make a container strong enough to hold the tension of honest conflicting thoughts and feelings. This does not mean that every rite has equal parts of joy and sorrow or gives each thought or feeling equal weight. But one cannot plan the ritual without knowing truly the weight of all the feelings Maureen and Rick are carrying, and without allowing honest tension to be part of the rite.

In our current dominant North American culture, the word *tension* usually has a pejorative connotation: tension is avoided; tense muscles hurt. Without critical reflection, even religious leaders tend to avoid or mitigate tension with strategies that may become unconscious, as if stress were bad. Cultural quips invite sliding over stressful situations, relationships, feelings, thoughts: "Get over it"; "No big deal"; "Just do it"; "Whatever." But actually, tension is what enables humans to walk and stand upright. Stress on bones makes them strong. The difference between "stress" (normal) and "distress" (not normal) is invisible.[8] Unfortunately, "tension" is usually uncritically judged to be distressful.

Falling into the "Avoid: too tense" category, then, have been such topics as lament, sin, and death. The cultural context makes it easy to deflect attention from unpleasant realities, and to avoid engagement with people, places, things, and ideas that one would prefer not to face. Families stand smiling in funeral receiving lines thanking people for coming. With the notable exception of some indigenous peoples, Christian rituals of remembrance of a death, on the one-month or one-year anniversary, for example, are rare. Rick is having difficulty facing the loss of his job. Both are having difficulty facing the tensive difference in attitude between them. This is a case of tension, indeed. Whether it finally will become a life-giving tension depends partly on the skill of the ritual maker. Rick is deep in the throes of lament. But the common experience and repertoire of lament is woefully limited in this cultural era. The challenge is to allow the depth of his lament and the height of her joy to abide together, in the preparation and then in the ritual, so that (like a concerto) honest hope may be celebrated at the end.

There are important worship resources for emotional honesty and holding conflicting feelings together in the great church traditions.

Hundreds of years of prayer and poetry, Scripture and song, have enabled such sensitive subtlety and tensive truth to be biblically and artfully expressed. All human life experience has ups and downs, joys and sorrows. This is the stuff of novels and artwork; lament and praise fill the pages of the Bible.

The churches have found one significant way to honor the highs and lows of life over a broader sweep, so that extreme joys and tragedies may be honored without a weekly emotional roller coaster. Through the seasons of the church year, supported by the Bible readings selected in common lectionaries for proclaiming and preaching in worship, the great changes in life tone can be honored.

For example, Lent is a time fitting for lament, sorrow, repentance, and confession. Like rainy days, it provides a sorrowful context for allowing one's sadness, guilt, anger, and depression to find expression, yet without sinking into it as a way of life. There is room for mourning and crying out. When the music and colors along with the Scripture and words set an inward context for self-examination and honest naming of pain and uncomfortable memories, it is easier for people to face such truths, without having to swim up a stream of "stiff upper lips" or "just do it." Something as simple as the pastor's insistence that at coffee hour during Lent only pretzels would be served (with coffee and juice) makes the point. One notices a difference. Together, simplicity is practiced. It helps.

In contrast, the unfettered joy of the Easter season can dramatize the opposite and allow sublimated joy to arise from the dead and shout freely. The church year, seasons of our salvation, makes a place for tensions in our affective lives where they can be received and honored with a *rhythm:* a seasonal rhythm in which each has its time, and all can be expressed.

How will the rhythm of Rick's and Maureen's contrasting tones be expressed ritually? Perhaps their ritual will need several movements. Perhaps some of Rick's friends will help him express his worry and self-deprecation, and his anger and frustration at Maureen, telling his story and finding Scripture and other writings to express his angst. Perhaps he would help write a prayer litany to enable him to lay it all on the altar of the Lord. Perhaps this ritual would be in one corner of the room, and Maureen and her friends may be in the opposite corner, witnessing.

In the second movement, perhaps Maureen's friends would help her do the same: tell her story and express what she sees and how she feels, and enable her to name her longing for Rick's dream fulfillment and the trapped sense of having had her hopeful insights considered unloving. Rick and his friends could witness this ritual.

Then perhaps the third movement, in which they approach one another, then stop, posing questions, expressing desires, perhaps yelling at first, dancing toward and away from one another. Bit by bit, the yelling becomes singing, the chaos turns to Scripture, perhaps some whimsy is included, and perhaps they repeat their marriage vows, as bit by bit, they move toward the center together. Perhaps a symbiosis in nature, two different creatures who give each other life, may be a defining metaphor. Perhaps, with the help of a caring and competent ritual leader, they may add new statements of avowal to their marriage vows, promises and assurances relevant to the vulnerable and creative moment in which they find themselves. The tension will keep them honest. The vows would assert union in its midst. Communion might complete this ritual.

The ritual being planned for Frank and Joanie would include the loss, the unraveling, of their marriage, yet also include thanks for what they had created together; some aspect of healing the pain between them; prayer to honor their now separate futures; and perhaps a new covenant to replace the marriage covenant. This is a wide range. The basic feeling-tone, however, would be one of lament. It would mark a new life of not-communion. On this occasion, there needed to be no main dish. And there needed to be a leader who could see this, and say it.

In Joanie's ritual, Barbara came to understand that after such a ritualized ending to the marriage, it would not be possible for the six of them to break bread as one body. Frank wouldn't want to be there; no one could have eaten. So she let go of the idea of a potluck, and gave herself to thinking of other ways to care for Joanie and Frank in this time.

So then, if there's no potluck at the end, no standard closure, how could Joanie's and Frank's ritual be ended? Would there be a way to finish such a ritual of ending or separation gently and send people off in separate directions without an abrupt stop or a forced communion? Here are some of the ways I imagine it could have been:

- They could have a reverse "unity candle"—one candle lit on the dining table, with two tall glass votives on either side, and two tapers. Each could lift a taper, light it from the single candle, then use it to light one of the tall votive candles. After extinguishing the tapers, together they blow out the single candle. Those who are there could ask God's blessing upon each of them, and call upon them to honor one another and their past with its gifts to each other, and to honor the future of each one's individual journey. Then they could each depart separately, even in silence, carrying the tall votive light with them, leaving several minutes apart or leaving by separate doors.

- Or there could be a prayer, perhaps one person giving thanks for all they have shared, and asking God's blessing upon the children and each of them, and guidance and strength to honor each other. Then the peace of Christ could be shared. Perhaps they could each receive one of the piles of thread, which would signify both the togetherness of the rite that honored the marriage and now its unraveling, and the individualism of their lives as now unwoven threads. Perhaps the women could retreat upstairs together as the men carried out the agreed-upon furniture or left the house with Frank. In this way they could still leave separately, in silence, perhaps.

- Or perhaps they could go out to the back yard, with the piles of thread. In a designated place, with a trowel handy, they could dig holes, and each place her or his wedding ring in the hole with some of the thread, and cover it over—and then scatter some seeds over the ground, that out of this death, something new may grow. Then with a closing prayer, they could in silence walk around the house to the driveway, and each drive away separately.

It's hard to think about. The ritual makes stark the reality—which *is* stark, and one doesn't want to face it—which is exactly why the rite is needed. Together, gently, through symbol and symbolic action, those gathered can enable the facing to happen. Ritual makes anguishing truth possible to face and to bear. The communion between them is broken, and this is sad. But thinking about it this way does make it *real*. There's no covering over here, no pretending that it's no big deal. It is a huge "deal." It is life shattering.

There must be hundreds of ways to end a separation rite in honesty without the standard potluck. The only definite is a closing prayer—for they must each leave with a prayer for God's blessing upon the children and all the fruits of this marriage, for each to continue to receive and live the gifts given, and for each to honor the other. A prayer. Something given and received as an enacted sign. And silence to hold the sad and sacred tenderness, the holy honesty, which the six of them, by the grace of God, will have witnessed.

Such grace occurred also at Vivian's ritual, thanks to Julia's response after her luncheon with Vivian. Vivian confirmed Julia's instincts: they would not dwell on the painful decades, for finally, this was a time of celebration; but they would not gloss over them, either. Julia created a flow that included the primary interaction of giving, receiving, and thanksgiving, inviting everyone to come and to bring a gift. At the event, the hospitable space and pattern was like what one would do at any baby shower: greeting guests, a place to put the gifts, offering drinks. Then there was a sequence of story telling and sharing food, for in this case communion was right and good, needed and longed for. There were tears and laughter. The gifts were sensitively selected: a birthstone bracelet with three stones, and a place to add the fourth. Storybooks for children that captured the poignancy of Vivian's circumstance. Gift cards to enable her to take Vicki out to lunch. A balloon that said, "It's a girl!" And there was a talking circle: a candle passed around, each one free to speak while holding the candle. Some women affirmed Vivian, how glad they were for her, how much they respected the way she was handling this. Others briefly shared stories of their own pains. The circle had started next to Vivian, so that she spoke last. This gentle structure created for her the space to tell more of her story, however much she wished, of loss and hope, pain and joy. There were words, symbols, action. Vivian later expressed her thanks for the ritual structure which was strong enough to express any joy or anguish that needed to be said, yet without expectation that she would respond in any particular way: "Thanks for your support and celebration, in such contrast to the loneliness I'd felt when I gave my baby up for adoption all those years ago. Thank you for this gift of freedom, and of peace."

Once empathetic listening reveals that creating a ritual is what will enable healing or transition for one of God's children, we have reflected upon *who* should participate (a community of ritual husbandmen and midwives). And we have identified two answers to the question of *how*: enacting a defining metaphor and engendering ritual honesty. Before concluding with *why* we do this—leading the baptized to the experience of resurrection living—we examine the third answer to *how*: mediating the labor of holy sacrifice.

5

Holy Sacrifice

Mediating the Labor Pains of Change

☙ Sometimes, simple is better. Sometimes, a supper of Chinese take-out enables the focus to stay on the conversation and the relaxing enjoyment without frenetic distractions like cleaning the kitchen, taking freezer inventory, remembering a recipe. Lowering tensions and expectations has become an art form (for example, "come as you are," "be casual," "whatever"). In many circumstances, this can be liberating and erase social stigmas. There is something to be said for the easy, the comfortable, and the convenient.

But there are other times when what really matters for human being (and also human *doing*) is not at all comfortable or convenient or relaxing; it can be the opposite of easy. Sometimes what really matters are inner attributes: vigilance, focus, attentiveness, empathy; or resisting envy and temptation, keeping faith, holding hope in the face of despair. Sometimes what really matters are outer actions: feeding the crying baby in the middle of the night, getting your homework (or project or sermon) done on time, speaking an unpopular truth, forgiving an unrepentant detractor, convincing the city to build a homeless shelter, living more frugally. Sometimes what really matters requires changing habits, becoming unpopular, changing priorities, no longer fitting in, living in higher purity and lower self-indulgence, being disciplined. In fact what really matters—being a disciple of Christ—can only be done with discipline. What really matters—following the Holy One through the Holy Spirit—requires holy living. What really matters costs everything. It takes sacrifice.

The irony is that when up against something ultimate, it will cost everything anyway. The question is whether it will cost everything and leave the person with pain and emptiness or whether it will cost everything and lead to life and hope. Joanie and Frank are facing a terrible loss that will cost them their dreams, their household, their family patterns, their married identity, and may cost them some friendships. However, if they do this ritual, the meaning of the losses may change. A bigger reality will be invoked, so that loss through divorce will be relativized and mitigated, and placed in relationship to that which is yet to come. A vision of future may grow larger and become as (or more) real than the empty present. In other words, no one can make the loss and pain disappear; but its power and meaning can be changed in the direction of life and hope or made to stand for something greater or turned to contribute to communion or thanksgiving. As one colleague put it, "We can't change the reality, but we can change the *experience* of the reality."

How? How can the meaning and experience of a reality be changed toward life? Through freely participating in the merciful fire of loving, self-giving sacrifice. The next principle for creating caring liturgies that are sanctifying and life giving is the focal person's wise and sensitive preparation for the rite to integrate inner agony with outer agony so that wholeness and holiness may be kindled. This integration gives the greatest gift—holiness—but first it costs everything. Joanie herself recognized its true name: sacrifice.

Every cultural mythology has a story of the sacrifice required for passage to another reality or to deep healing. Joseph Campbell catalogued numerous such stories and called them "the hero's journey."[1] In Christianity, Jesus first withdrew to the temple at age twelve, leaving the ordinary to encounter the holy and finding his true authority in the home of his Father. Later, at age thirty, he was cast into the desert where he was utterly emptied through terrible temptation, and weakened by lack of food. Holding firm to his core by the power of the Spirit, however, Jesus integrated even these assaults by the Tempter into a deeper strength and compassion, through which he led disciples, changed the world, and continues to lead two millennia later. A presage of the cross, his desert labor cost him dearly. If he had given in to the temptations, where would we be today? His endurance, a gift of the Spirit, came out of his character, but also out of a tremendous effort. His own suffering was huge. He was different after the desert. He was ready for his ministry. This was a laborious sacrifice for him. It enabled the fulfillment of *his* life and ministry; but see how it also made possible *ours.*

A Brief Christian Midrash on Sacrifice

"Sacrifice" is a confusing word for Christians. On the one hand are apparent exhortations *not* to sacrifice. Jesus says directly to the Pharisees (in perhaps an irritated voice), "Go and learn what this means: 'I desire mercy, and not sacrifice'" (Matt. 9:13a). Earlier, Amos had proclaimed the word of the Lord: "Even though you offer me your burnt offerings and grain offerings, I will not accept them. . . . But let justice roll down like waters . . ." (5:21-24; cf. Mic. 6:6-8). And since Jesus made the ultimate sacrifice for us on the cross once for all, Christians understand themselves to have been freed from such sacrifice.

But on the other hand, Paul wrote, "Present your bodies as a living sacrifice, holy and acceptable to God, which is your spiritual worship" (Rom. 12:1). And since Christians are supposed to follow Jesus who sacrificed his life, aren't they to do the same? Christians seem to be exhorted both to avoid sacrifice and to offer *hesed* (steadfast love, mercy), "living sacrifice," as part of "spiritual worship." It's confusing and controversial.

Clearing the confusion is helped by looking at the word itself, *sacrificio,* which means "to do holiness." In the Latin, *sacr–, sacer + facere,* we have a root meaning "sacred" and a verb meaning "to make" or "to do," as in "fashion." To sacrifice is to fashion sacredness—to actually *do it.* It is active. It means to participate in making holy, in being holy, in putting our bodies about doing holiness. Christians (Jews, too: see Exod. 31:12-13; Lev. 11:44-45; 19:2; 20:7-8, 26; 21:6, 8, 23; 22:9, 16, 32) are most certainly supposed to live in holiness, to grow in sanctification. In order to grasp how sacrificing the tablecloth and how Grace's sacrificial labor will participate in holiness in their ritual, let us take hold of two shifts in traditional understandings of sacrifice: that blood sacrifice is not essential to "get right with God," and that holy sacrifice is to be freely offered and not exacted: an outpouring *given,* not taken. Understanding each in turn will help rite makers know how to create ritual to bless participants.

From Sacrifice of Blood to Sacrifice of Compassion and Praise

The earliest peoples understood that ultimate powers were at work in the universe, and that relating to them in harmony required blood: that is, the very life of something. Spilling blood would make right relationship with the gods. But not the random spilling of anyone's blood. Rather, a proper offering to God must be one's best and most valuable. And what is more valuable than one's own child? In the earliest days, then, this was the blood that would best make right relationship with God. In the days of human sacrifice, the most valuable person was a son that opened the womb, a "firstborn son." The story of the binding of Isaac (Gen. 22:1-19) seems to indicate that God was calling for an end to such human sacrifice. That a pure, unblemished animal (in this case, a ram) could be substituted for a human offspring would have utterly transformed relationship with God! The terrible human fear, the need to appease, the wrenching conflict between love of God and love of family, would be eliminated. This generous God gave the human family new peace.

However, there were still all those animals sacrificed, and there was a lot of blood (Num. 28:3-31). Morning and evening, an animal was sacrificed on the altar in the temple to keep the whole covenanted people in right relationship with God. And this doesn't count the sin offerings, guilt offerings, and thanks offerings—grain as well as animals—individuals might offer. Blood must have flowed everywhere. The primary question of the prophets and Jesus, however, was, Did these bloody sacrifices actually accomplish a right relationship with God? In addition to their theological effectiveness and power, did the people's hearts change? Were they living in the freedom of right relationship that the sacrifices were intended to effect? Was it *working*?

Some of the prophets seemed to think not. Hosea, for example, spoke the Lord's words to the people: "For I desire steadfast love and not sacrifice, the knowledge of God, rather than burnt offerings" (Hos. 6:6, RSV). Hosea writes in the style of Hebrew parallelism, in which the meaning of the first line is repeated in the second. "Sacrifice" here, then, refers to "burnt offerings." The Lord is calling the people to a shift in focus, from the practice of burnt offering sacrifice to *hesed*, lovingkindness, compassion, mercy, which is the knowledge of God. It is Hosea's words that Jesus tells the Pharisees to go look up and to follow (Matt. 9:13a).

In other words, the point of the burnt-offering sacrifices in the first place was never just to *do* them. It was to do them *in order to help one's heart to turn,* as a sign of sorrow and repentance, as a sign of willingness to make a change in one's life to live more as God wants, so as to be in right relationship with God. Burnt-offering sacrifice was intended to be an outward sign of the inward change of heart.

But the difficulty with any regular activity is that legalism creeps in. The practice can be done without thinking. Pretty soon it can be done by rote with no thought at all of its intention. It can become a checklist. This is a natural tendency for human beings.

Certainly, the practice has its effect on the body and the unconscious, even if the person is not fully engaged. Keeping the practice helps keep faithfulness through grueling or tortuous times. The very benefit is the habit and pattern of it. The problem can come when the purpose behind the practice has been lost, or when the ministry of the body has been utterly disconnected from the prayer of the heart so that one fails even to notice that neglecting a person in need is a violation of prayer.

Most of us have "said" the Lord's Prayer with our lips without our minds ever noticing what the words meant, without our hearts or bodies in a prayerful attitude at all—paying "lip service." It's legalism: performing the law for its own sake and not as a means to its spirit. Jesus and the prophets hated this. Empty rituals were anathema. Actions with no meaning, outward with no inward, letter with no spirit over a period of time are rote, empty, dead. A right relationship with God leans toward being fully alive, awake, alert, present, paying attention, and, yes, integrated so that body, mind, heart, and soul are all meaning and expressing the same thing. It seems that Hosea and Jesus want integrity—the spirit and the letter together. But when they find them separated, either rote ritual action with no compassion, or compassion with no ritual action, they shout the message that compassion is what matters. The point of the ritual in the first place was to enable the person to move into holy living and into the compassion of God.

From Sacrifice of Something Else to Sacrifice of Self

The big wrinkle in sacrifice for Christians, however, comes at the cross. The whole sacrificial system involved taking the life of one of God's creatures, spilling its life blood, in order to be right with God. On Calvary, however, Jesus preempted the whole need to take a life—because Jesus gave a life: the one life he had the power and freedom to offer—his own.

Blood was spilled, but it was one's own—a self-gift, in freedom, and in love. In loving and pleading for forgiveness for his very executioners, Jesus poured out his own life. This has "made right" the relationship of the whole human family with God forever.[2]

Jesus *gave* his own life, as a gift, freely. And this gift was returned to him (and to us) unexpectedly at the resurrection. What a sacrifice that is! Yet when given freely out of love, such a self-giving sacrifice is holiness. It gives life and changes everything. And those who are baptized into Christ's death and resurrection receive Christ's self-giving,[3] and in gratitude are covenanted into this very pattern of death and life. The baptized become part of the circle of self-giving, which is thanksgiving, which is love and freedom.

For at Pentecost, the Spirit descended not just upon one person but upon the whole people. The Spirit of Holiness did not transfer from Jesus to one other person, or from Christ the great high priest to another priest. No, the Holy Spirit descended upon all the people gathered, the *priestly people* (1 Pet. 2:9-10), called and baptized, covenanted and sent, to be Christ's body in the world. Grateful for the gift of God in Christ and the Spirit, this people would carry on Christ's ministry for the kingdom, pouring themselves out freely in love and forgiveness, for the life of the world. We have not stopped doing holiness or making sacrifice or emptying ourselves as Christ did. On the contrary, in thanksgiving for our oneness with Christ, we are covenanted to continue.

Done out of gratitude and in the spirit of utter compassion, acts of lovingkindness and intercessory prayer and worship are sacrifices of praise and thanksgiving, which cost everything, but which we are able to offer freely. These are gifts, not wrested from us, but our privilege, our covenant, our ministry, our living in the reign of God in the now. At the supper of the Lord, the Eucharist, some denominations articulate the people's offering of themselves—"our souls and bodies," as one text put it[4]—as a participation in the power of Christ's self-giving sacrifice then, still operating now.

Therefore, in Christ sacrifice has not ended but changed. The making of holiness, sacrifice, is still a Christian vocation in imitation of Christ: but generally not blood (unless one's own), and not wrested but offered freely. Christians are given, rather, unspeakable freedom to receive Christ's compassion and power, and in the spirit of gratitude, to give a tithe of thankful self-emptying, in worship and in life. Sacrifice is about doing this; but it is also about being this: the priestly people, the holy people, the mediators of this love and this freedom wherever they gather together. Because for Christians, baptized into Christ, sacrifice *is* mercy.

Labor as an Expression and Integration of Holy Sacrifice

When a baby is born, the mother is said to go through labor. This is an interesting term, since the mother is not selecting a work or job in the sense of a day laborer. Rather, the mother's labor is a response to and participation in the initiative of her body and the baby's coming. Yet the mother's involvement is physical and painful. Riding the wave of the baby's rhythm requires pushing very hard sometimes, and avoiding pushing at other times. Part of what the mother labors at is endurance. To get through the experience, she needs a coach, a guide, an encourager. It is both a communal effort with coach and midwife or physician, and it is uniquely her experience, effort, endurance, and agony. It is hard work. It is labor.

Labor is also required on the other end of life. Dying is not easy. It helps to have a coach, a death-midwife such as a hospice worker, who knows the process and can guide the person through the stages to the next world. At the same time, the effort to make peace with one's life, with all that was done and left undone, reconciling, blessing, accepting, letting go, preparing, and embracing: this can only be done by oneself. It is both helped by a community, and done uniquely on one's own. But through this labor, something new is created: the old is passing away, and lo, a new creation is being born into the nearer presence of God.

A new reality is not born without a gift of the Holy Spirit, without inspiration, without the descent of the Holy Muse. But holy inspiration alone is insufficient for the creation of a new identity, relationship, church, world, self. Labor is needed. In Genesis 1:1—2:4a, even God labored for "six days" to make creation. Jesus did not promise his disciples a burden-free life. To the contrary, he promised a certain character to the burden: "My yoke is easy and my burden is light" (Matt. 11:30). There is indeed a yoke; there is a burden. But it is not an oppressive burden or deadening or too heavy to carry. It is instead to be carried in freedom and joy, with ease of spirit. It is a yoke freely borne with lightness of heart.

Understanding that passage and healing and holiness require labor and sacrifice, ritual makers are willing *to call the focal person to fitting travail so that the rite can be true.* Like the priest in the film *The Mission* who matched the soldier's laborious penance to the soul-depth of his sin, like the pastor or sponsor who requires the hard work of making amends before the rite, competent rite makers are unafraid to help focal persons name and accomplish the honest sacrifice needed (and to accompany or midwife them through this labor). When the need for sacrificial effort is neither acknowledged nor engendered, the focal person may be subjected to a ritual that provides merely "cheap grace," as Dietrich Bonhoeffer describes it—a pseudo-reception of God's grace not worked fully into the dough of a person's life. A curt nod toward the idea of God's grace given in sacrificial love on the cross and mediated through the resurrection may be a theological acknowledgment, but may not result in a heart of flesh or experiential power or changed living. Ritual makers must not deny the fire of God's love, which only changes human persons if they freely open themselves to becoming a new being, tempered in its heat. As Augustine puts it:

> This bread signifies to you how you ought to love unity. It was made out of many grains of wheat, which were separate, but were united by application of water, by a kind of rubbing together, and baked with fire. So have you been ground together by the fast and the exorcism, wetted in Baptism, and baked by the fire of Christ and the mystery of the Holy Spirit. . . . Notice how at Pentecost the Holy Spirit comes: He comes in fiery tongues, to inspire the love whereby we are to burn towards God and despise the world, and our chaff be burnt away, and our heart refined like gold. So the Holy Spirit comes—after the water the fire—and you are made bread, which is the Body of Christ: and here is the symbol of unity.[5]

Joanie took the initiative on her own, as did Grace, to labor over a new creation in service to the ritual honoring Joanie's loss and preparation for a new station in life. They had only a week in which to complete their respective works of unraveling and writing a poem. In this case, the deadline itself created a container, an oven, in which the fire of energy and creativity could give rise to a temperature not tolerable on a day-to-day basis. The ritual is extraordinary, a holy time-space other than "business as usual." But the ritual is not the only holy part. The preparation—the time and planning and prayer and labor that occurs before the rite—is also essential for the work of the ritual to be fulfilled. Unraveling and creating were holy opportunities for sacrificial change, for outpouring of friends' love, for kneading of Joanie's spirit, so that in the ritual oven she might receive the fullness of God's grace.

A ritualization, like baptism, is a way of marking and enabling a reality that is ready to be born. That is, the ritualization is not the first thing that is done, but is the climax, the completion, in order to make way for the next beginning.

For example, typically one does not marry someone after one date, or even three very good dates. A marriage is a lifelong commitment. The shift from single to married utterly changes a lifestyle. Every pattern—social, emotional, problem solving, decision making—will be changed. What enables a marriage to work is that the changing begins long before the wedding, so the couple gets a sense of whether and how they can work together and how their partner operates. While most of the changing will happen after the wedding, the ceremony is a moment in a continuum or process well begun. In arranged marriages where the couple meet at the wedding ceremony so that no collective changing occurs in advance, unless gender roles are strongly established, it can take many more years to function as a partnership. One needs time and preparation to adjust to the other, to know the other, to plan lives in tandem.

And one of those preparations is preparing for the wedding, the ritual, itself. In the process of that planning, the couple continues to learn more about each other and their families, to experience more problem solving and decision making, and to make social and emotional changes. There is labor and sacrifice needed to be able to climb over a stile or into a ferry. Without the energy, the courage, the muscle tone, it cannot, in fact, be done.

A further example of preritual preparatory sacrifice, including the need for the labor of work, effort, and struggle on the part of the focal person to accomplish the passage they seek comes from nature. If a chick does not get out of its eggshell, it will, of course, die; for it keeps growing, and the shell finally squeezes it. But it is not just *being* out of the shell that matters. It's the process of pecking out. The chick must expend the baby labor of pecking in order to live. But pecking is hard work. Even with the special hook on the front of the chick's beak that helps it peck through the hard shell, the chick must labor. It is possible for a chick to lack the strength to peck through. However, when experimenters "helped" chicks by gently opening the shells for them so they didn't have to work so hard, they discovered to their chagrin that the chicks soon died of weakness. The sympathetic lab workers had deprived the chick of the very exercise it needed to live those next few days outside the shell. As hard as the chicks must work to free themselves from the shell, this very labor is a gift for their life. The same is true of butterflies struggling out of their cocoons. Others easing their way is their death penalty. The struggle is the means of life.

Preceding the ritual action with preparation that involves appropriate labor or exertion can make a big difference in the meaning, value, and power of the ritual action to the focal person. Sometimes there is a tithe of the labor carried over in the ritual itself, a symbol of the preparatory work, as there was when Joanie and Frank, with their friends, completed the unraveling together. The ritual is not the place for major time-consuming labor, however. Rather, a ritual is a container holding only so much. It is an event with a beginning, a middle, and an end. The primary labor happens before the rite. What can happen during the ritual, then, is a symbolic offering of that labor, and a giving of thanks to God for its completion and for its part in the healing or passage.

Ritual action is not magic, but is a moment in a process, marking an ending or a beginning, or often, both. It animates and makes real—tangible, visible—the affections, relationships, commitments, desires, and turning that have been in process in the person's life. Ritual leaders who help the vulnerable recipients concentrate some of those changes in preparation for the ritual, so that they can be gathered up and represented in the ritual action, help focal persons both to recognize and participate in the work God is doing in their lives. Jesus' effort to resist temptation in the desert was the very preparation needed for his new ministry.

The process before the rite can be liberating and empowering by involving the person in her or his own process, with the ritual as a goal or end. Sometimes it's more possible for people to do needed work when they know there's a celebration or end point or purpose to which their hard work is leading. Their labor will be consummated. And the consummation of this labor will be a Christian caring liturgy. The sacrifices offered before and even during a liturgy can be understood as a participation in the paschal mystery of Christ.

Just as Jesus' spiritual labor in the desert was essential before beginning his self-sacrificial ministry, so the sacrificial effort preceding rites of passage and healing is essential to make way for new ministries the Spirit can open for all the baptized as a result of such life crises. God's redeeming work in Christ turns dead-end fences and lakes into life-giving stiles and ferries, leading to new paths, new shores, new life—and thus new possibilities for ministry. Such rituals, when they make room for such sacrifice, participate in God's redemption.[6]

Joanie's persistent labor to unravel the tablecloth marked an end to the marriage—but where in the ritual will the hope be expressed for a new beginning? Without such hope and redemption patently manifest, it would not be a Christian ritual, for worship and all Christian ritual engages and enters a primary symbol of the faith—the paschal mystery of Christ, the subject of the next chapter. Hope and redemption can be spoken in words, but are often expressed most deeply in labor that leads to art. The promise of new beginning, like the passion of Christ, is something given, offered, accomplished. Making beauty participates in redemption, and requires effort as well as inspiration. I end this chapter with a primary sign of such redemption: a work of art created for Joanie's ritual. Grace "listened" deeply in heart-listening attunement to Joanie's process and grasped the laborious sacrifice and effort she was putting into her ritual. Grace wrote this poem, read toward the end of the ritual, which celebrated Joanie's labor as participating in the radiant result of Christ's passover: resurrection. I share this poetic fruit of Grace's labor of love, with her permission:

> She is spending her days
> In deconstruction.
> Dismantling the tablecloth
> That for ten years of their twenty-eight
> Was spread across the kitchen table.
> The idea came quite suddenly, with instant recognition.
> This needed to be done—
> The desolate unweaving of the cloth.
>
> It had been the kitchen's center,
> Focal point,
> Heart of home.
> Draping the round table,
> Welcoming all entrants.
> But everything has changed now
> And she knows this must be done:
> The resolute unweaving of the cloth.

Its pattern is a reassuring plaid,
With woof threads white and yellow,
And warp of warm fiesta shades:
Pink and aqua,
Lilac, yellow-green.
She separates these tenderly
and goes about the work:
The tedious unweaving of the cloth.

She invites her friends to help her,
Offers insights and advice.
The first threads are the hardest, she assures us.
This she has discovered to be true.
And certain threads are disinclined to move,
Requiring coaxing, teasing, firmer grasp,
But by and by they come more easily,
The flowing tears begin to dwindle,
And you settle to your task:
The bittersweet unweaving of the cloth.

We sit around the table, working quietly as one,
This table where we've sat for years and years
While eating vegetarian cuisine,
Critiquing plays we've just enjoyed,
Decrying current news of war,
Laughing over stories of the kids,
And crying sometimes, too.
Now we sit together
For the serious unweaving of the cloth.

Methodically we place each thread
With color-coded kindred.
Some stretch out long as single strands,
Recalling tautness, maybe nestled close
In memory.
But others—the recalcitrant, perhaps? the unresolved?—
Re-curl, recoil, return to fetal place,
Refusing to pretend
To live again.
We handle each with reverence and respect
As we participate
In the powerful unweaving of the cloth.

She is not Penelope,
Quite opposite, in fact.
She unweaves not to keep alive the hope
That her lover will return,
But to make concrete the fact
That her life with him is gone.
And thus she goes about the work
The desperate unweaving of the cloth.

Again, unlike Penelope,
She does not unweave at night, in secrecy, alone,
but publicly, in daytime, in the company of friends.
She invites him over, even, with a group of us
To share in the final, heart-wrenching, stages of the work.
She asks us all to take some threads,
Encouraging him too.
From her threads she'll create a work of art,
Something new,
Its form not yet determined.
Embracing one another now, we take our leave;
Pausing at the door to see her sitting there, intent,
Finishing the work at hand,
The radiant unweaving of the cloth.

6

The Paschal Mystery
The Crux of Caring Ritual

This book has so far offered five principles for creating rituals of healing and transition so that churches can enable those baptized into Christ to grow and mature in his likeness. In the current post-Holocaust and now post-Christendom time, it is critical that every person baptized into Christ, at whatever age, be tended and supported to become ever more holy, alive, and Christ-like, in being and in acting. Called to be a "little Christ" (*alter christus*), every baptized person is avowed and covenanted to live and love in the freedom to which Jesus called his disciples and in the reign of God for which Christ's body is formed.[1] Could Christ's ministry truly be fulfilled if only the ordained participated? No, Christ calls us all, seeks the building up of the body, sends us into the world to love and serve in Christ's name. Would not Christ's ministry thrive if not just the ordained, but if all those covenanted to Christ in baptism were maturing in Christ and living out their calling to Christ's ministry in the world? It is the role of the churches, which have a stake in the maturing of every baptized Christian, not only to conduct Sunday worship, preach, teach, and inspire, but also to learn, teach, and practice the conducting of personal rites of healing and passage with life-giving competence.

Centerpiece of Christian Living:
The Paschal Mystery of Christ

The sixth principle that this chapter offers turns toward the beginning of the baptismal process, which is also the why (goal, purpose) of Christian ritual action: the paschal mystery of Christ. It is from this and for this mystery that all the other principles are engaged in a commitment to caring ritual for the vulnerable ones who need it. We end at this principle of the paschal mystery for four reasons. First, a Christian ritual maker engages the paschal mystery as the lens through which to look at the focal person's life, to see the ways God has already been at work saving, healing, and redeeming, even if hidden from awareness: it is the lens to one's life in Christ. Second, the paschal mystery of Christ is also the paschal mystery of those whose lives are bound to Christ, who are part of his body, covenanted to live and serve as he did: it is the call and commitment focusing the baptized life. Third, essential for ritual competence, the paschal mystery is the very basis for Christian ritual, to assure that any personal healing liturgy connects with an ultimate concern: it is the critical criterion for Christian ritual. Finally, this mystery of the passover from death to life is a movement from Good Friday to Pentecost: it is the spirituality of the baptismal process of growing and being carried from dead end to new beginning throughout the Christian life. To comprehend these four roles, it is important to be refreshed as to what exactly this "mystery" is.

As the centerpiece of the Christian faith, paschal mystery refers to the stunning incomprehensibility—the *mystery*—of Jesus' *pasch* or passover from death to life, from crucifixion to resurrection. For Jesus, it was the ultimate passage. He passed from life to a painful death in self-giving love. But this was only the first half. The disciples were incredulous at the second half: his passing over from that death to new life in resurrection on the third day. This mysterious passover of Christ resulted in an inversion of power, not only then, but ever since. Then, now, and to come, death is defeated by love, and a holy freedom is available by means of shifting focus away from pain and self, and toward goodness and lovingkindness for others. The mysterious part is not only *that* it happened and *how* it happened, but also how it is that any of the rest of us can *participate in it*.

To follow Jesus is to walk into this paschal way of being. It's not easy. Willingness is necessary, but willingness alone won't do it. And frankly, a lot of tempered character has to develop for most of us to be willing to put our own gain aside for another or for the common good. "Mystery" is a good name for this. None of us can live this paschal way of being alone. It takes the grace of God, and everything we are, and the care of the community of faith, including caring liturgies.

The point of Christian rites is to help make apparent the focal persons' connection with Christ, so that they can acknowledge their own paschal deaths and celebrate God's gift to them of a new, resurrected life with a new spirit. Christian ritual is spiritual. Christian ritual making is a liturgical practice, and also a theological practice; but it is foundationally a spiritual practice. It is the essence of the baptismal process because it invites the Holy Spirit to deepen the connection of our deaths with Christ's death, and thus our lives with Christ's life, made manifest not only in Sunday worship, but also in particular rituals of passage and healing for every person united with Christ in baptism.

As we have seen, both passage and healing involve dying, or in Arnold Van Gennep's first stage of passage, "separation"—a letting go, a detachment, an ending, a goodbye: to one's youth, to the single life, to the married life, to one's vocation, to health, to dependence, to victimhood, to pain, to dreams, to failure. These are little deaths, and dying is a spiritual experience which (of course) includes the body.

This chapter will help caring ritual makers more fully grasp the way in which the paschal mystery of Christ (and, derivatively, the body of Christ, the church) is the source, the means, and the end of Christian ritual through its role as process from Good Friday to Pentecost, as lens for recognizing God's work, as call of the baptized, and as critical ritual criterion. We begin with an ending account of Joanie's story from Grace's husband David, one of the two couples who participated in Joanie and Frank's ritual. Although there was no designated ritual leader for this rite, Dave sensed the need to begin the ritual by making a connection with the paschal mystery. Following his liturgical and spiritual sensibilities, he took the initiative to lead the first part of the ritual.

This was very painful and hard. Of course, I didn't want to see them divorce. Grace told me about the unraveling, and I didn't want to go at first, but then I agreed. And I started thinking. I had the sense that there needed to be some kind of context, some ritual action or symbol or something.

I'm involved in liturgy at my church, and so I began to think about how we might create an atmosphere of renewal, starting over, starting again, fresh start, and I thought of the ritual of baptism. Then I thought about the house, which is going to be there for a while, that Joanie would be there, that all the memories would be there. So I thought we should do something in relationship to the house, perhaps a ritual cleansing of the house of all the bad stuff. We couldn't do the whole house, but we could do the front door—remembering the angel of death passing over.

So I had everyone gather just inside the front door, and I began to say in a prayer-full way about what wonderful memories this house held, in this family that had existed to this point—and that this day we wanted to cleanse the house of all the bad memories, and leave only the original grace and goodness that was at work all those years. So I began to wipe the jambs and lintel and the doorknob with a plain white cloth, and I walked to the opening to the living room and wiped that entry as well. I invited people to help and passed the towel around, and we wiped the hallway and all the openings that opened out of it.

Then Joanie took over, and we were given the plaid tablecloth pieces. As we sat at the dining table, we told stories. We'd all sat there at that very table for many dinners, especially after we'd gone to the theater together. At first it was quiet, except for discussion about how best to unravel the cloth. It wasn't easy work and we struggled; eventually we got the hang of it. Then, after a while, we did some genuine sharing. It was very good, although Frank may not have talked at all.

At the end, Grace read a poem she had written. Then Joanie gave each one a wad of the unraveled colored thread. We all hugged, and Joanie cried.

We stood around by the stove, not wanting to leave (since that was the end). Frank had fixed the stove, this was the first time he spoke, he was finally drawn into it. He was the first to leave after that. He hadn't brought a truck, and he didn't take any of the furnishings with him.

Then the rest of us left together, and out of Joanie's earshot began to talk, to share how sad it was. I was pretty emotional by that time. I was sad, angry. It was so difficult to see them part ways. And I couldn't eat—I was just too heartsick.

There were gaps in this ritual, in that there was not a leader aside from Joanie to lead the planning or the rite, Frank was not drawn more fully into the planning, and the ending had not been thought through. Had a leader been available who understood all the principles discussed here, the rite may have been more peace making and fulfilling for all the participants.

However, even without conscious awareness of these principles of Christian ritual making, the formation of the Christian people does create a certain ritual fluency, which is why the conscious creating of transition and healing rites makes sense as a natural gift Christians could offer in the world. Conscious awareness will help. In this case, for example, no one asked Dave to do what he did in the opening cleansing of the doorways of the house. He just saw a need—a critically important need—and had the imagination and confidence to fulfill it. In response to questions about his role, he said:

In the midst of this painful brokenness, I thought, Why not respond with symbolic activity? The wiping, washing, cleansing was a sign of our frustration, our struggle. What we did—the opening in the front hall, and then the unraveling at the dining table—really seemed to help in the long run, and not just Joanie, but us. It was such a loss for all of us.

People ought to have more of that—to help you cope. It's also a way of turning from the gods who don't exist, and honoring the One who does exist. Ritual is so helpful because it transforms the voltage so people can stand what's next.

Dave was really torn up about the divorce because of its moral implications, because of the pain that two very close friends were having to endure, and because of his own loss. For it wasn't just the couple who were breaking up; it was the community of couples, and the possibility of continuing patterns like evenings at the theater preceded by dinner and followed by conversation.

But even in his own pain, he was able to recognize and hold in himself the goodness and creativity that had been part of this marriage, and the hope we have in a trustworthy God, who showed us through Christ that death which is part of passage to new life is paschal, not dead-end.[2] Dave had the spiritual depth and ritual fluency to know that something more than the unraveling of a marriage needed to be symbolized for the ritual to be whole. Even in this simple beginning, with little preparation, Dave helped them honor the house, which symbolized their family and life together, with reference to the waters of baptism, which are cleansing and forgiving, giving birth to new life. He invited them to participate in preparing the doorways for new entrances and exits, for new passages. Or, as Grace put it, he took "symbolic bucket and cloth, cleansing the home of sorrow room by room."

And, strikingly, he brought his own awareness of two significant truths, stated in his last two sentences. In the midst of his own loss and anguish, Dave recognized that ritual action "transforms the voltage so people can stand what's next." This ritual marking of divorce was a hard and final reality. In this case it was necessary and true, but that did not change the difficult unraveling emptiness of it. Trying not to look at the pain and finality of divorce may be instinctive; but avoidance would not make it go away. And in fact, ritualizing it makes it manageable, opening up to Christ's redeeming work. The ritual makes it possible to be in the midst of the loss with Frank and Joanie so that there could be togetherness even in the midst of the separation. This ritual enacted the reality that, on a deeper level, the friendship and care Frank and Joanie had shared would always underlie whatever conversations or silences they experience over the years. Not only that, to do this with their friends made possible a way of sharing and connecting together in spite of, and deeper than, the loss. Dave's metaphor is a good one: the ritual lowers the voltage so that the people can handle devastating agonies together, in truth, without denial. They have physically touched it, and the wad of unraveled fibers is smaller than they are.

Dave's second insight, one he himself helped mediate, was daring to turn toward our God, even in sin and pain and failure and loss. Confession is strength. Lifting broken pieces to the Lord is an act of courageous hope. The cultural gods of "Get over it" and "Just move on," or "You know how men are" and "Women make no sense" are not the God Christians proclaim Sunday by Sunday. But in turning toward the God we proclaim, such small half-truths become (blessedly) impossible. Not only that, the God we proclaim became incarnate in Jesus Christ, who preemptively gave his life for others, and rose again. Even in his quiet, simple way, Dave led this small group of caring, hurting friends into a manifestation of the paschal mystery. There is always the washing. There is always a new door to walk through. This house, holding so many memories, so much life and now death, is proclaimed a paschal house in Christ, washed to prepare for the new life the Spirit is preparing to come.

1. Paschal Mystery as Ritual Spirituality of Baptism

The paschal mystery, then, is the crux—the cross, the intersection, the heart—of Christian ritual, because it is the lens by which to see life as those baptized into Christ are called to live it; it is the call and commitment of those covenanted to Christ at baptism; it is the standard or critical criterion by which the appropriateness of conducting a Christian ritual (or not) is gauged; and it is the spirituality of the baptismal process, in which we come to live, teach, and affirm our lives as lived in cycles from Good Friday to Pentecost. We address this fourth facet first. According to priest and retreat leader Ronald Rolheiser, "The paschal mystery is the mystery of how we, after undergoing some kind of death, receive new life and new spirit. Jesus, in both his teaching and in his life, showed us a clear paradigm for how this should happen."[3]

In his marvelous book *The Holy Longing,* Rolheiser invites Christians to penetrate the meaning of "Christian spirituality."[4] In his chapter on the paschal mystery, he reminds a culture too easily dismissive of "unhappy thoughts of death" that no philosophy or anthropology or psychology or spirituality "can pretend to be mature without grappling with the timeless, haunting questions of suffering and death. These are realities that gnaw at the heart."[5] They are endemic to the human condition; but how we handle them has everything to do with the condition of our humanity. He calls the paschal mystery "a cycle for rebirth," but he acknowledges that this can be confusing unless people are clear what "death" means and what "life" means. His distinctions are helpful.

There are two kinds of death, Rolheiser says: *terminal* death and *paschal* death. "Terminal death . . . ends life and ends possibilities. Paschal death, like terminal death, is real. However, paschal death . . . while ending one kind of life, opens the person undergoing it to receive a deeper and richer form of life."[6] He refers to John 12:24: "Unless a grain of wheat fall into the ground and die, it remains only a single grain; but if it dies it yields a rich harvest. . . . There are also two kinds of life: . . . *resuscitated* life and . . . *resurrected* life." To be restored to one's former life, as Lazarus was (John 11), is to be resuscitated. To be given a new life altogether, from which one "would not have to die again," is to be resurrected.[7] "The paschal mystery is about paschal death and resurrected life."[8] It is a process of moving through the first in order to receive the second.

Insightfully, Rolheiser also distinguishes between *life* and *spirit.* They are not the same, and they do not come at the same time. We are given life before we are given the spirit for that life we are already living. On the road to Emmaus, the disciples had been given a new life in freedom through the resurrection. But they could not recognize Jesus among them, because they had not yet let go of the former reality in order to receive the spirit for their new life and freedom. At Pentecost, the disciples were given the Spirit for the new life they were already living.

Rolheiser summarizes the paschal movement in terms of the church's theological calendar:

1. Good Friday: "the loss of life—real death"
2. Easter Sunday: "the reception of new life"
3. The Forty Days: "a time for readjustment to the new and for grieving the old"
4. Ascension: "letting go of the old and letting it bless you, the refusal to cling"
5. Pentecost: "the reception of new spirit for the new life that one is already living"[9]

Rituals of Christian spiritual care, as we are discussing them, occur most appropriately when persons are nearing the point of Ascension or Pentecost in their situation. The purpose of these rituals is to help them move to the fullness of new life with a new spirit. Helping them pass all the way through to Pentecost is the place and purpose of creative Christian ritual. To make a clear connection with "personal, paschal challenge[s] for each of us," Rolheiser states the paschal movement this way:

1. "Name your deaths"
2. "Claim your births"
3. "Grieve what you have lost and adjust to the new reality"
4. "Do not cling to the old, let it ascend and give you its blessing"
5. "Accept the spirit of the life that you are in fact living"[10]

When Vivian (chapter 4) was contacted by her birth daughter, Vicki, she was somewhere around "Ascension." Her "forty days" had been almost thirty years long; she had grieved; she had let go of all the dreams related to her daughter—but she had not received a blessing. Vicki's telephone call itself created a recapitulation of this process, bringing to life again the terrible loss, yet also the "Easter" of being found by her daughter and being able to recount her grief to her women's group. What was needed in a ritual was an acknowledgment of Ascension and a carrying toward Pentecost. What a ritual could do was enact the letting go, mediate blessing, and enable her to claim the spirit for the life Vivian was living: the mother of a daughter she did not know, whom she had not raised, who did not live with her, but whom she loved with all her heart, and to whom she could now show that love. It was a new spirit of forgiveness (which would be part of the blessing), thanksgiving, and hope for a relationship far into the future.

If Vicki herself had had a community of ritual midwives, they might have identified her stage as "just before Ascension," unable to let go of the fear that perhaps her birth mother didn't love her, but hopeful enough to find out. Had they provided a pastoral ritual for Vicki, they may have offered a two-part rite: something simple as she prepared to meet an unknown mother for whom she longed but by whom she may have felt abandoned, and then a ritual after their first meeting, when it was clear whether the tone should be lament or joy. In this case, after meeting Vivian, that finding of love would have opened the way for both blessing and new spirit to be celebrated with abundant joy.

The "deaths" Rolheiser names would be fitting for consideration of healing and transitional ritual: the death of our youth, our wholeness, our dreams, our honeymoons, and certain ideas of God and church.[11] A new spirit does not always come automatically. Sometimes it does, because of the person or the circumstances or wise counselors or loving families or chance. When it doesn't come, then what? Then it is an occasion for Christian ritual.

This is why ritual honesty is crucial. Letting go is loss. It can feel like death. It requires lament and sackcloth and ashes. It deserves tears and anger and sorrow. But even the pain visited upon us must bless us. Like Jacob wrestling with the angel, an angel he would not release without its blessing (Gen. 32:24-30), Rolheiser claims that we, too, must allow ourselves to receive a blessing from the past—including the wretched past—before releasing it to ascend. We are all wounded; yet we have all received *something* from the very ones who have wounded us. "No matter how bad your father and mother may have been, some day you have to stand by their graveside and recognize what they gave you, forgive what they did to you, and receive the spirit that is in your life because of them. Making peace with the family depends upon proper mourning and letting the ascension and pentecost happen."[12]

The paschal mystery, then, is the spirituality of the baptismal process by which those covenanted to God live day by day in Christ, living into little deaths and resurrections, and leaning into receiving the Holy Spirit in ongoing Pentecosts. Christian ritual makers can play an important role in spiritual-ritual guidance for life-giving passage and healing for one another.

2. Paschal Mystery as Lens Through Which to See Life

The paschal mystery is also a lens through which one looks at the focal person's life, to see the ways God has already been at work saving, healing, and redeeming, even if hidden from awareness—for this is the shape of one's very life in Christ. That is, those who live a Christian world view see the world through kingdom eyes and recognize God's creative and redemptive work everywhere around them. Over time, as one deepens in sanctification, or *theosis* (that is, becoming more and more God-like), it becomes less and less possible to view a situation outside God's presence, action, and grace.

A pastor or spiritual guide, then, listens with the questions, Where are death and resurrection already extant? Where do they need to be made apparent? Looking through the lens of the paschal mystery, she or he seeks signs of death, especially unarticulated death (fear, anxiety, shame, guilt, anger, powerlessness, victimization, alienation, and so on), and also signs of resurrection (hope, accomplishment, freedom, life, new beginnings, possibility, maturation, deeper God-centeredness, justice, mercy, purity). Empathy and heart-listening are essential, and then naming what is heard and checking its veracity with the person(s).[13]

For example, one man, an only child, had been abused and over-controlled by his mother and neglected by his father. He grew up isolated, with a low view of himself, and spent much of his energy in self-deprecation, even hitting and hurting himself when things didn't go right. It was as if the mother he had escaped now lived inside him so that he himself had taken on her voice, yelling at himself constantly for his stupidity, even in situations that went well or for which he had no actual responsibility. Thus this man complained and disparaged everything about his life and his circumstances.

When his wife threatened to divorce him, he finally went to a spiritual guide who asked him how God had been working in his life. "I don't know where in the world God is!" he cried (Good Friday). With gentle questions and spiritual exercises over time, the spiritual guide led him to see how God had helped him escape from his childhood home, had given friends and mentors who poured themselves out for him to give him an excellent education, had made sure he was never destitute, had provided for him even in bleakest times, had given him a life companion in his wife whom he adored, had enabled him to find his current job at which he was a success, and had given him three children and several grandchildren. Then the spiritual guide pressed him to find ways to offer thanks-gifts to God, a practice unfamiliar to him, which he at first resisted. Gently, however, over time, he began to soften, and to notice the generous grace all around him (Easter). At that point, then, the spiritual guide suggested they plan a ritual of thanksgiving and freedom, marking a turning from the emotional/psychological enslavement of most of his life to the new-found freedom now possible in the years remaining to him (acknowledging forty days and moving toward Ascension). This wise spiritual guide helped the man see not only the deaths in his difficult life, but also the constant, ongoing, grace-filled gifts of life bestowed on him over the years by the Holy Spirit.

That is, Christians understand the paschal mystery as foundational to being human. Rite makers, seeing by faith persons' journeys as paschal, can walk with them even to the depths of emptiness and seek signs of the ongoing blessing of the Holy Spirit in their lives. Such spiritual conversations begin the process of ritual making.

3. Paschal Mystery as Both Call and Commitment of the Baptized

The paschal mystery of Christ is also the paschal mystery of those whose lives are bound to Christ, who are part of his body, covenanted to live and serve as he did. It is the call and commitment of the baptized.

The invitation to live in the kingdom or reign of God is an invitation to see differently. Mistakes, endings, failure, sin, hate, evil, and death are all in process of redemption by our God. This God calls people to covenantal relationship, to participate in the processes of creation and redemption. To enter this covenant is to commit to freely living in the realm of God and to see, understand, and live redemptive deaths as Jesus did in order also to participate in creative, redemptive life, in oneself and with others. It is a life of self-giving love, which is a dying to self, in order to truly live. The paschal mystery is a way of life and a way of liturgically, ritually, and spiritually interpreting and celebrating life for God's covenanted people.

Every leader of worship, including of sacraments and creative rituals discussed in this book, needs to be vigilant in making ways for worshipers to bring their lived experience[14] of participation in the death and resurrection of Christ to the body's liturgy as an offering and a thanksgiving to God. Filled, then, with the Holy Spirit, the people are able to continue to live this covenanted, Christ-like way. By the Holy Spirit, worshipers are liberated to stand for truth and speak with courage and without fear. Focused on Christ, fear and loss are reduced bit by bit from primary status to background colors. This is the sacrifice of praise and thanksgiving, the sacrifice of "ourselves, our souls and bodies."

There are many examples in Scripture of God's covenanted people pouring themselves out in ways that risk physical death—or other kinds of death emotionally or relationally—in love for others. Nathan, the prophet, for example, was the messenger bringing the unfortunate truth to King David (2 Sam. 12:1-15); such messengers were not always treated kindly. The widow who gave the last bit she had, risked going hungry the next day (Mark 12:41-44). Queen Esther stretched courageously beyond what were traditional women's limits to intercede for her people (Esther). Joseph risked his reputation in taking as his wife a woman already pregnant (Matt. 1:18-25; Luke 1:26-56). All these were called by the Lord to these actions, which were foolish, and thus direly risky, in their human communities.

There are also numerous examples in the news of committed persons following God's call irrespective of risk. Corrie Ten Boom tells a World War II story of hiding Jews behind a false wall in their Dutch Protestant home, and then, when she herself was arrested by the Nazis, she made the agonized decision to leave behind her carefully packed prison bag because she feared drawing attention to that false wall it was resting against.[15] It is a story of risky, preemptive giving. It is the paschal mystery; it is a way of life for giver and receiver; and for Christians, it is call and commitment.

Persons enter the paschal mystery at their baptism, when they are united with Christ in his death and resurrection.[16] The washing of baptism signifies death to one reality and birth to another, as Paul states so exquisitely in Romans 6:3-4: "Do you not know that all of us who have been baptized into Christ Jesus were baptized into his death? Therefore we have been buried with him by baptism into death, so that, just as Christ was raised from the dead by the glory of the Father, so we too might walk in newness of life."

In baptism, Christians are thus united with Christ's paschal mystery. Their identity changes, and they become part of his body, members of the church (1 Corinthians 12). God was incarnate in Christ; this mystery continues in the *ecclesia*, the living body of Christ on earth. The incarnation of God in Christ, active in the Spirit, frames a space for human Christ-likeness; the covenant of baptism starts the process.

It is our own experiences of resurrection, in life and in worship, that make us free to risk death for another. All worship celebrates this mystery: Sunday liturgy, Holy Communion, weddings, funerals, other creative rituals—all of it.[17] The Last Supper was the beginning of Jesus' passover, his *pasch*, and Christians participate in Jesus's action anamnetically every time they celebrate the sacrament. But other rituals, too, involve death and life. In marriage, one dies to one's single life to be born to a new community with another in faithfulness all one's days. Funerals, honoring the death of a beloved, are services of resurrection, celebrating the sure and certain hope for all the baptized and all God's people that we will rise with Christ in the fullness of time. Joining a religious community represents a death to one kind of life in order to be born to another. It is appropriate to ground ritual movement in Christ's *passover* from death to resurrection so that the call and commitment of God's people to a paschal life can be manifest in healing and passage by God's great act of redemption in human history through the power of the Holy Spirit. Even more strongly, if there is no participation possible in the paschal mystery, then a situation is not a fitting subject for a Christian ritualization.

4. Death to New Life as the Critical Criterion

The paschal mystery is a criterion for Christian ritual, to assure that any pastoral liturgy is of ultimate concern. Indeed, it is the very basis for Christian ritual. Therefore, thinking paschally can be critically important in considering whether a situation is appropriate for a Christian ritual.

For example, a creative pastor, realizing the need for Christian rites of healing and transition, developed three rites and posted them on his web page: one for high school graduation, one for the death of a pet, and one for a divorce. To his surprise, the divorce rite got the most downloads, with the pet funeral second, and the high school graduation the least. The situations most in need of a rite were the two involving some kind of death. Divorce is an instance of failed covenant, which is most certainly a kind of death. While it is not evil, it does fall in the category of sin, which needs healing, forgiveness, and reconciliation, which those who are divorced cannot give themselves, and which is the very purpose and result of Christ's death and resurrection. A rite of divorce has a very different tone than a rite of marriage, certainly. But it can raise the truth of the finality and death of the marriage covenant and confess it honestly. Forgiveness can be given, and a new covenant can be entered into: for example, to honor their new status, to work peaceably together for their children, parents, and friends, to avoid slander of each other, and to hold dear their good memories and all that they have created together. This *is* the paschal mystery.

Pets serve as surrogate family members for many people, and while not the same as human family, they are often loved and cherished as family members. Their loss may create deep grief, which could well be mitigated by the comfort of a rite honoring the death of one of God's creatures. The death of a family member of whatever species is, literally, a death.

But high school graduation, while indeed a letting go, is not itself an instance of the paschal mystery. Although there is a dearth of puberty or maturation rites (and some would suggest that this is one reason for protracted adolescence), the high school graduation does not represent a Christian ritual need.[18] For one thing, there is already a rite in place: commencement or graduation. When done well, this fulfills the need to help make the transition from one stage and situation (high school education) to the next (college, job, independence). It is an ending as well as a new beginning (that is, "commencement"). Graduation is a good stile over the fence of this transition for the student. This transition for the teen typically does not involve death or grief, and the loss is usually minimal, since it is usually possible to keep in contact with friends and favorite teachers. The "death" for the student is small, though the parent may feel differently. For the student, high school graduation is not finally a passage from death to life but from life to life, a success leading to a kind of promotion. While the student's church family may celebrate with a gift or meal, this is not a fitting occasion for a full ecclesial ritual: it is not paschal.

Yet when such cultural moments seem to be the only signs of passage to adulthood available, many church folk assume that these are the moments the church should celebrate. And the sensibility that something is needed is correct. Recognizing the paschal mystery as primary criterion for Christian ritual, however, enables pastors to discern which moments the church would be involved in to support young people in the true passage they are facing, in Christ. A pastor or spiritual guide might begin with whatever is given, including cultural symbols such as driver's licenses and car keys, letters of job offer or college acceptance, or even high school diplomas, but then use them as part of a deeper symbol system of the death of childhood (innocence, certain freedoms) and the birth or claiming of adulthood (responsibility, sacred trust, social covenant).

The core of such work is for the ritual guide to search out the paschal mystery in a situation, to help the focal persons identify the roots of vulnerability and need, to listen for and name the temptations and deaths that are blocking them, and to help them be open to the Spirit's work of turning the terminal death into a paschal death. Competent and creative ritual makers listen and watch for death and life, raise this to the focal persons' awareness, and guide them into a ritual in which their deaths can be experienced in terms of Christ's death, and they can be drawn into hope in resurrection to new life.

So the primary criterion for such Christian ritual is that the inherent death and resurrection in a situation be identified and then made evident in any ritual. Once the deep issue and ritual need is found, it may be that a rite exists that can be used or adapted for the focal person.

Because the paschal mystery is central to Christian life, it is normal for pastoral persons to look always deeper. And because this paschal death becoming resurrected life is central to being human, the way to find the presence of God hidden in someone's life is to seek it. It is pastors' and ritual-makers' work to seek, to find, to recognize, and to "name grace."[19]

But if there is no existing rite, it is the work of the churches to create one. To creatively place radically particular personal circumstances in relationship to God's gifts of resurrection and Pentecost, imaginative Christians must lead people into Christian rituals custom-designed to mediate God's loving them from death into new life. Ritual making is a necessary and appropriate practice for Christian pastors. It is a liturgical, theological, and spiritual practice with pastoral application. Compassion and competence are essential.

The death and resurrection of Christ has given humans freedom to continue living after leaving behind the self-indulgence of childhood, the identity as one who is victimized or incapable, the devastating loss of divorce, death, or loss of one's home with its memories to a hurricane or tornado. The sixth principle, then, is to seek the paschal mystery at work in focal persons' lives, and to offer Christian rituals in relationship to those situations of ultimate concern in which their spirits need support for passing through death to new life in Christ.

Conclusion

All humans encounter situations that bring them to the edge of the abyss. Then what? It is hard to know what to do. But one thing we do know: Christ's life, death, and resurrection changed forever the meaning of the abyss. The church is at its strongest when the human family faces death; for this is the very identity of the ones called Christian. All those covenanted in Christ at their baptism need to know that this is the mystery they live, and they need the guidance and support to live this holy mystery moment by moment, year by year.

At the edge of the abyss, words are needed, but not too many words. Silence is needed, but not too much. Aloneness is needed, but not too much. Togetherness is needed, but not too much. Caring action is needed: letters, touch, casseroles, thoughtfulness. Symbols are needed: flowers, people, things, actions. Scripture is needed, and theology, and meaning. And to make one event of all these requires integration.

Ritual engages story, symbol, and action to integrate one person's life with the cosmic flow of God's ongoing creation and redemption. Working below the level of conscious awareness, ritual does not explain but enacts the real. Words reach their limit.[20] Communal action in ritual's safe "container" can hold any crisis in the context of salvation history and the paschal mystery. It is powerful; therefore, it is serious. Ritual matters; it makes a difference. Shallow ritual makes a shallow difference and can trivialize the situation or, worse, the church's worship. Competent ritual can free. It can ferry persons across to a healthier shore or be the stile of passage from one life situation to another. When spiritually, fluently, and competently done, ritual can care for someone's mind, body, and soul. And the practice of regular caring ritual for those marked with the cross of Christ at baptism can enable a vibrant laity, an active *ecclesia,* spreading Christ's ministry throughout the world. When spiritually, fluently, and competently offered, ritual is a pattern that can turn chaos and pain into healing stillness.

May the Spirit of God bless all who engage in this good work.

Notes

Introduction: Worship as Ritual

1. Grimes's book of essays, *Beginnings in Ritual Studies* (Lanham, MD: University Press of America, 1982) carved out the field and began the process of generating new knowledge. While not a discipline with its own methodology, ritual studies is, however, a field with a wide range of contributors, especially from the disciplines of anthropology, sociology, history of religions, and religious studies.

2. A few books that open up the relationship between worship and pastoral care include Herbert Anderson and Ed Foley, *Mighty Stories, Dangerous Rituals* (San Francisco: Jossey-Bass, 1998); *Religious and Social Ritual: Interdisciplinary Explorations,* ed. Michael B. Aune and Valerie DeMarinis (Albany: State University of New York Press, 1996); Elaine Ramshaw, *Ritual and Pastoral Care*, Theology and Pastoral Care (Philadelphia: Fortress Press, 1987); and William H. Willimon, *Worship as Pastoral Care* (Nashville: Abingdon, 1982).

3. Catherine Bell, *Ritual Theory, Ritual Practice* (New York: Oxford University Press, 1992).

4. Bell says, "[Stanley] Tambiah shares with many other ritual theorists a concern to show how ritual communication is not just an alternative way of expressing something but the expression of things that cannot be expressed in any other way." Ibid., 111.

5. "Symbolic rupture," a term from Louis-Marie Chauvet in *Symbol and Sacrament* (Collegeville, MN: Liturgical, 1995), 330–39, will be developed more in ch. 3 in the discussion of symbol.

6. For a helpful example that contrasts the Christian eucharistic meal with an ordinary meal, see Bell, *Ritual Theory,* 90–91.

7. Paul Tillich, *Dynamics of Faith* (New York: Harper & Bros., 1957), 42, 43.

8. Bell borrows the term *misrecognition* from Pierre Bourdieu; see *Ritual Theory,* 82.

9. Jerome W. Berryman, *The Complete Guide to Godly Play: An Imaginative Method for Presenting Scripture Stories to Children*, 4 vols. (Harrisburg: Morehouse Continuum, 2002); see esp. vol. 1 for his method for presenting the lessons so that children's focus is held.

10. See the video presentation by Thomas G. Rogers, *Turning Ink into Blood: Resources for the Public Reading of Scripture* (St. Paul: Seraphim Communications, 2001).

11. Bell, *Ritual Theory,* 83–85.

12. This term derives from Suzanne G. Farnham, et al., *Listening Hearts: Discerning Call in Community* (Harrisburg: Morehouse, 1991); they use "focus person," which they attribute to the Quakers (78).

13. William Bouwsma, "Christian Adulthood," in *Adulthood*, ed. Erik H. Erikson (New York: Norton, 1978), 81–96. "Manhood" lauds reason and unchangeability as humanity's zenith (thus tending to deny full humanity to women). "Adulthood" (from *adolescere*) values maturing (Heb. 6:1).

14. See James Fowler's *Stages of Faith: The Psychology of Human Development and the Quest for Meaning* (San Francisco: Harper & Row, 1981). For the assertion that "intentional faith development" is essential in the life of a vibrant congregation, see Robert Schnase, *Five Practices of Fruitful Congregations* (Nashville: Abingdon, 2007), 59–78.

15. Theologians have used various terms to describe this becoming God-like: divinization (*theosis*—Irenaeus); deification (*theopoiesis*—Athanasius); deiformity (Aquinas); sanctification (Wesley, et al.; cf. 1 Cor. 1:30; 1 Thess. 4:3-4; 2 Thess. 2:13; 1 Pet. 1:2)

16. See in particular Matthew Linn and Dennis Linn, *Healing of Memories* (New York: Paulist, 1974).

17. Ronald Grimes, *Ritual Criticism* (Columbia: University of South Carolina Press, 1990), 191–209.

18. See Theodore Jennings's article "On Ritual Knowledge" in which he shows the knowledge gained from that which is consistent in repeated rituals, and from that which changes (for no two rituals are ever exactly alike); *Journal of Religion* 62, no. 2 (April 1982): 111–27.

19. For more information on the catechumenate process, see Alan Kreider, *The Change in Conversion and the Origin of Christendom* (Harrisburg: Trinity Press International, 1999), 24.

20. Edward Yarnold, *The Awe-Inspiring Rites of Initiation* (Collegeville, MN: Liturgical, 1994), ix. Yarnold says these rites are more aptly called "spine-tingling."

21. Grimes, "Infelicitous Performances and Ritual Criticism," in *Ritual Criticism,* 191–209.

22. I derive this term from Roland Delattre's term "ritual resourcefulness" ("Ritual Resourcefulness and Cultural Pluralism," *Soundings* 16 [1978]: 281–301), and from Regis Duffy's term "symbolic competence," in *An American Emmaus: Faith and Sacrament in the American Culture* (New York: Crossroad, 1995), 118.

23. For example, see Rebekah L. Miles, *The Pastor as Moral Guide*, Creative Pastoral Care and Counseling (Minneapolis: Fortress Press, 1999).

24. The four biogenetic stages that are part of the life cycle of any living being are birth, maturation, reproduction, and death. Human cultures mediate these biological stages through their own sets of rituals. Arnold van Gennep named these *rites de passage,* and identified three stages in each passage: separation from the prior identity (e.g., child, single person), liminality (the neutral zone in between), and reaggregation into the community with the new identity (e.g., adult, married person). See van Gennep, *The Rites of Passage,* trans. Monika B. Vizedom and Gabrielle L. Caffee (Chicago: University of Chicago Press, 1960 [1909]).

25. On the relationship between story and ritual, see Herbert Anderson and Ed Foley, *Mighty Stories, Dangerous Rituals* (San Francisco: Jossey-Bass, 1998).

Chapter 1: Creative Rites

1. Herbert Anderson and Ed Foley, *Mighty Stories, Dangerous Rituals* (San Francisco: Jossey-Bass, 1998).

2. See Isabel Florence Hapgood, compiler and translator, *Service Book of the Holy Orthodox-Catholic Apostolic Church, arranged from the Old Church-Slavonic Service Books of the Russian Church and Collated with the Service Books of the Greek Church,* 6th ed. (Englewood, NY: Antiochian Orthodox Christian Archdiocese, 1983).

3. See especially S. Mary Anthony Wagner, OSB, *The Sacred World of the Christian: Sensed in Faith* (Collegeville, MN: Liturgical, 1993).

4. International Commission on English in the Liturgy, *Book of Blessings,* study ed. (Collegeville, MN: Liturgical, 1989).

5. See the *Book of Occasional Services* (New York: Church Hymnal Corp., 1979).

6. *The Book of Common Prayer* (New York: Church Hymnal Corp.), 411ff.

7. This term is inspired by Elaine Ramshaw's exceptional book *Ritual and Pastoral Care*, Theology and Pastoral Care (Philadelphia: Fortress Press, 1987).

8. Karen B. Westerfield Tucker uses this term in "Creating Liturgies 'In the Gaps'," *Liturgy* 22, no. 3 (2007): 65–71.

9. Of the several important books in this field, see, for example, Teresa Berger, *Women's Ways of Worship: Gender Analysis and Liturgical History* (Collegeville, MN: Liturgical/Pueblo, 1999); Marjorie

Procter-Smith, *In Her Own Rite* (Nashville: Abingdon, 1990), and *Praying with our Eyes Open* (Nashville: Abingdon, 1995); Susan K. Roll, et al., eds., *Women, Ritual and Liturgy* (Leuven: Peeters, 2001); and Rosemary R. Ruether, *Women-Church* (San Francisco: Harper & Row, 1986) for the early call to attend to women's rites and women's liturgical leadership.

10. This material is taken from my article "Rites of Healing Along the Baptismal Journey: An Example and Several Principles," *Liturgy* 22, no. 3 (2007): 49–56.

11. "Human Situations in Need of Ritualization," *New Theology Review* 3, no. 2 (May 1990): 36–50. In-text citations refer to pages in this article.

12. These terms come from Sally F. Moore and Barbara G. Myerhoff, "Secular Ritual: Forms and Meanings," the introduction to their book *Secular Ritual* (Amsterdam: Van Gorcum, 1977), 3–24, esp. 10–15. See also Michael B. Aune, "Introduction," in *The Return of the Worshiper to Liturgical Theology: Studies of the Doctrinal and Operational Efficacy of the Church's Worship*, unpub. ms. (Berkeley: Pacific Lutheran Theological Seminary, 1992), 3–10.

13. Moore and Myerhoff, "Secular Ritual," 12.

14. *Baptism, Eucharist and Ministry*, Faith and Order Paper No. 111 (Geneva: World Council of Churches, 1982), vii.

15. Ibid., "Baptism," I.§1.

16. These, as well as being made part of Christ's covenanted people (the church), filled with the Holy Spirit, and participating in this sign of the kingdom of God, are the five meanings of baptism ecumenically agreed upon. Ibid., II.§2-7.

17. Moore and Myerhoff, "Secular Ritual," 12–13. Emphasis added.

18. This material comes from Susan Marie Smith, *Christian Ritualizing and the Baptismal Process: Liturgical Explorations Toward a Realized Baptismal Ecclesiology* (Eugene, OR: Wipf & Stock, 2012), chap. 1.

19. *Adelphopoiesis* was a Byzantine rite for the creation (in the eyes of society and church) of a household of unrelated persons. Byron David Stuhlman, *Occasions of Grace* (New York: Church Hymnal Corp., 1995), 86–89.

20. Empathy is essential in the process of ritual making. However, there is a risk that some would-be rite makers may believe they have empathy, but instead may be projecting their own needs upon another. The distinction between *empathy* and *projection* is a crucial one. See *The Dictionary of Pastoral Care and Counseling,* exp. ed., ed. Rodney J. Hunter (Nashville: Abingdon, 2005), "Empathy," 354; and "Projection," 960.

21. Susan Marie Smith, "Worship as Loving God and School for Loving Neighbor," in *Loving God, Loving Neighbor*, ed. Sondra Higgins Matthaei (Kansas City: Saint Paul School of Theology/Xlibris Press, 2008), 61.

22. But see Kenan Osborne's important work *Christian Sacraments in a PostModern World: A Theology for the Third Millennium* (New York: Paulist, 1999).

23. See Valerie DeMarinis, *Critical Caring: A Feminist Model for Pastoral Psychology* (Louisville: Westminster John Knox, 1993), on the importance and function of ritual and symbol to engender experiences of caring, and to strengthen hope for the future, esp. 42–43.

24. See James Fowler, *Stages of Faith: The Psychology of Human Development and the Quest for Meaning* (San Francisco: Harper & Row, 1981).

25. Megory Anderson, *Sacred Dying: Creating Rituals for Embracing the End of Life* (New York: Marlowe, 2001), xx–xxi.

26. Penelope Wilcock, *Spiritual Care of Dying and Bereaved People* (Harrisburg: Morehouse, 1996), 4; in ibid., 20–21.

27. Anderson, *Sacred Dying*, 18.

28. Ibid., 22. Emphasis added.

Chapter 2: Ritual Midwives

1. "Maieutic" (from Greek) is the adjective for "midwife." While mediating and coaxing to birth is a good metaphor for rite making, I intend it to refer to both men and women in the way "husbandry" might be done by both genders.

2. This is one of the "liturgical gaps" Karen Westerfield Tucker addresses in her article "Creating Liturgies 'In the Gaps,'" *Liturgy* 22, no. 3 (2007), esp. 67–71.

3. This is also true of newly generated nonreligious ritual. A movement called Gather the Women (http://www.gatherthewomen.org/gtw/index.htm) spawns gatherings all over North America.

4. This case is recounted in its entirety in my article "Rites of Healing Along the Baptismal Journey," *Liturgy* 22, no. 3 (May 2007): 49–56.

5. Ibid., 54.

6. This simple yet profound truth comes from my *Doktorvater*, Louis Weil.

7. On liturgy and ethics or the Christian moral life, see *The Journal of Religious Ethics,* 7, no. 2 (1979) focused on this topic, including Don E. Saliers, "Liturgy and Ethics: Some New Beginnings," 173–89; Paul Ramsey, "Liturgy and Ethics," 139–71; and responses to these. See also *Liturgy and the Moral Self: Humanity at Full Stretch before God,* ed. E. Byron Anderson and Bruce T. Morrill (Collegeville, MN: Liturgical, 1998), esp. Gordon Lathrop, " 'O Taste and See': The Geography of Liturgical Ethics," 41–53; and Don E. Saliers, "Afterword: Liturgy and Ethics Revisited," 209–24; also Saliers's essays, "For the Sake of the World: Liturgy and Ethics," in *Worship as Theology* (Nashville: Abingdon, 1994), 171–90; and "Pastoral Liturgy and Character Ethics: As We Worship So We Shall Be," in *Source and Summit,* ed. Joanne M. Pierce and Michael Downey (Collegeville, MN: Liturgical Press, 1999), 183–94. Saliers cites Stanley Hauerwas, *Character and the Christian Life: A Study in Theological Ethics* (San Antonio: Trinity University Press, 1975).

8. Elsewhere I have called this "Engagement of Christian Worship Patterns and Symbols," since the sequence and structure of any rite are the matrix of meaning it conveys; "The Scandal of Particularity Writ Small: Principles for Indigenizing Liturgy in the Local Context," *Anglican Theological Review,* 88, no. 3 (2006): 385–86.

9. Saliers, "Afterword," 219.

10. "Constitution on the Sacred Liturgy" (December 4, 1963), II.14, in *The Documents of Vatican II,* ed. Walter M. Abbott (New York: The America Press, 1966).

11. See Ernst Käsemann's book by that title: *Jesus Means Freedom,* trans. Frank Clarke (Philadelphia: Fortress Press, 1969).

12. See Rosemary Radford Ruether, *Women-Church: Theology and Practice* (San Francisco: Harper & Row, 1986).

13. See, for example, Teresa Berger, *Women's Ways of Worship: Gender Analysis and Liturgical History* (Collegeville, MN: Liturgical/Pueblo, 1999).

14. In addition to ibid., see also, for example, *Wising Up: Ritual Resources for Women of Faith in their Journey of Aging,* ed. Kathy Black and Heather Murray Elkins (Cleveland: Pilgrim, 2005); Lesley A. Northrup, *Ritualizing Women: Patterns of Spirituality* (Cleveland: Pilgrim, 1997); and Susan Starr Sered, *Women as Ritual Experts: The Religious Lives of Elderly Jewish Women in Jerusalem* (New York: Oxford University Press, 1992).

15. For one excellent process to help discern who may be called to this work, see Jacqueline McMakin with Rhoda Nary, *Doorways to Christian Growth* (Minneapolis: Winston, 1984), esp. the last course of six sessions, 184–241.

16. See Thomas G. Long, *Accompany Them with Singing: The Christian Funeral* (Louisville: Westminster John Knox, 2009) on the need for depth in Christian funerals. The very title demonstrates that funerals are not *just* for those left behind, but is the last part of this life's journey for the deceased.

17. See, for example, Susan Marie Smith, "Bridging Death and Life: An Alaskan Athabaskan Funeral Experience," *Liturgical Ministry* 7 (1998): 9–22.

18. "Thick description" is Gilbert Ryle's term, quoted by Clifford Geertz in "Thick Description: Toward an Interpretive Theory of Culture," in *The Interpretation of Cultures* (San Francisco: Basic, 1973), 3–30; here, 6–7. Thick description describes not only actions, but their contextual meaning.

19. For more on the importance of perspective taking, see James Fowler, *Stages of Faith: The Psychology of Human Development and the Quest for Meaning* (San Francisco: Harper & Row, 1981), 73–79, 244–45.

20. Herbert Anderson and Edward Foley demonstrate this in recounting the evolution of an Italian American family's holiday rituals in *Mighty Stories, Dangerous Rituals* (San Francisco: Jossey-Bass, 1998).

21. Don Saliers calls the latter "remembering the world to God." See his books *Worship and Spirituality* (Philadelphia: Westminster, 1984), 86; and *Worship as Theology: Foretaste of Glory Divine* (Nashville: Abingdon, 1994), 126–36.

22. Kathleen D. Billman and Daniel L. Migliore, *Rachel's Cry: Prayer of Lament and Rebirth of Hope* (Cleveland: United Church Press, 1999), 65.

23. Louis-Marie Chauvet, *Symbol and Sacrament: A Sacramental Reinterpretation of Christian Existence* (Collegeville, MN: Liturgical, 1995), 134.

24. See E. Byron Anderson, *Worship and Christian Identity: Practicing Ourselves* (Collegeville, MN: Liturgical, 2003).

25. Don Saliers has drawn back into conversation the important spiritual ethical need to cultivate inner emotional orientations, which Jonathan Edwards called "affections." Saliers's work on the religious affections, such as joy, gratitude, and repentance, can be found in *A Soul in Paraphrase: Prayer and the Religious Affections* (New York: Seabury, 1980); awe, delight, truth, and hope are discussed in his *Worship Come to its Senses* (Nashville: Abingdon, 1996). See also Jonathan Edwards (1703–1758), *A Treatise on Religious Affections* (Grand Rapids: Baker, 1982).

26. See Henri Nouwen, "A Self-Emptied Heart: the Disciplines of Spiritual Formation," *Sojourners* 10 (August 1, 1981): 20–22.

Chapter 3: Metaphors and Symbols

1. See Ronald Grimes, *Deeply into the Bone: Re-inventing Rites of Passage* (Berkeley: University of California Press, 2000).

2. Ibid., 336, 342.

3. Ibid., 343.

4. Mary Gerhart gave this simple and memorable expression of how metaphor works in her presentation on hermeneutics at the University of Notre Dame in 1992; cf. Mary Gerhart and Allan Melvin Russell, *Metaphoric Process: The Creation of Scientific and Religious Understanding* (Fort Worth: Texas Christian University Press, 1984).

5. For example, see Paul Ricoeur, *Interpretation Theory: Discourse and the Surplus of Meaning* (Fort Worth: Texas Christian University Press, 1976).

6. William Bridges, *Managing Transitions: Making the Most of Change* (New York: HarperCollins, 1991).

7. These are Don Saliers's words. See his description of the intercessory prayers of the people as "Remembering the World to God," in his *Worship and Spirituality* (Akron, Ohio: OSL Pubs., 1996 [1984]), 69–78; and his *Worship as Theology: A Foretaste of Glory Divine* (Nashville: Abingdon, 1994), 126–36.

8. This distinction comes from my essay "Worship as Loving God and School for Loving Neighbor," in *Loving God, Loving Neighbor,* ed. Sondra Matthaei (Kansas City: XLibris, 2008), 60–75.

9. "Theological Reflection Method," in *Education for Ministry* (Sewanee, TN: University of the South, annual updates). Contact: School of Theology Programs Center, The University of the South, 335 Tennessee Avenue, Sewanee, TN 37383; (800) 722-1974; efm@sewanee.edu.

10. The classic book on the relationship between ritual and play is by Johan Huizinga, *Homo Ludens: A Study of the Play-Element in Culture* (London: Routledge & Kegan Paul, 1980, 1949). See also David N. Power, *Unsearchable Riches: The Symbolic Nature of Liturgy* (New York: Pueblo, 1984), 84–87.

11. Haim Ginott describes this phenomenon from a psychological perspective in *Between Parent and Child* (New York: Avon, 1956), 43–59.

12. See Zalman Schachter Shalomi, *From Age-ing to Sage-ing: A Profound New Vision of Growing Older* (New York: Warner, 1995).

13. Susan Marie Smith, "Rites of Healing Along the Baptismal Journey: An Example and Several Principles," *Liturgy* 22, no. 3 (2007): 51–52.

14. Rainer Maria Rilke: "My life is not this steeply sloping hour in which you see me hurrying. Much stands behind me: I stand before it like a tree; I am only one of many mouths, and at that the one that would be stilled the soonest. I am the rest between two notes that are somehow always in discord because Death's note wants to climb over; but in the dark interval, reconciled, they stay there trembling; and the song goes on, beautiful." *Selected Poems of Rainer Maria Rilke: A Translation from the German and Commentary by Robert Bly* (New York: Harper & Row, 1981), 30–31.

15. According to Clifford Geertz, the "only way meanings can be 'stored' is in symbols." See "Ethos, World View, and the Analysis of Sacred Symbols," in *The Interpretation of Cultures* (New York: HarperCollins, 1973), 126–41, at 127.

16. See Ricoeur, "Metaphor and Symbol," chap. 3 in *Interpretation Theory*. Page numbers in this section refer to this volume.

17. Ibid., 50.

18. Ricoeur opposes "a substitution theory" of metaphor—one word or image for another—in favor of "a tension theory of metaphor" in which "new signification emerges." *Interpretation Theory*, 52, 55.

19. Symbols "are intrinsically related to what they express; they have inherent qualities (water, fire, oil, bread, wine) which make them adequate to their symbolic function and irreplaceable. . . . A sacramental symbol . . . participates in the power of what it symbolizes, and therefore, it can be a medium of the Spirit." Paul Tillich, *Systematic Theology*, vol. 3: *Life and the Spirit; History and the Kingdom of God* (Chicago: University of Chicago Press, 1963), 123.

20. "The symbol is the smallest unit of ritual which still retains the specific properties of ritual behavior; it is the ultimate unit of specific structure in a ritual context." Victor Turner, *The Forest of Symbols: Aspects of Ndembu Ritual* (Ithaca: Cornell University Press, 1967), 19.

21. See Ronald Grimes's chapter on ritual failure or "infelicity" in *Ritual Criticism* (Columbia: University of South Carolina Press, 1990).

22. Louis Weil's description is valuable: The "sacramental principle: to see God in all created things. In other words . . . God is revealed in the whole created world; and in that sacramental perspective, everything is understood as an access, or a transparency, to the presence and action of God. . . . [O]rdinary things can be instruments of grace; . . . an object, a physical, created object can bear the holy, can be an instrument or means of grace. . . . The sacramental sense is not narrowly Christian because it is grounded in a certain understanding of our humanity." Transcribed lecture, Church Divinity School of the Pacific, Berkeley, Feb. 8, 2000. Elsewhere, Weil writes that sacraments "reveal that the physical world, far from being evil, is the domain of God's activity" (and therefore physical objects and actions can mediate encounter with God). *A Theology of Worship* (Cambridge: Cowley, 2002), 17.

23. *Caro cardo salutis:* "The flesh is the hinge on which salvation depends." Tertullian, *On the Resurrection of the Flesh,* chap. 8, para 1; http://www.newadvent.org/fathers/0316.htm.

24. Even more, Theodore Runyon shows that the creation itself is the foundational sacrament, the *ursakrament.* See his "The World as the Original Sacrament," *Worship* 54, no. 6 (1980): 495–511. See also Edward J. Kilmartin, "A Modern Approach to the Word of God and Sacraments of Christ: Perspectives and Principles," in *The Sacraments: God's Love and Mercy Actualized,* ed. Francis Eigo (Villanova: Villanova University Press, 1979), 59–109.

25. Lawrence Hoffman, *Beyond the Text: A Holistic Approach to Liturgy* (Bloomington: Indiana University Press, 1987), 174, passim: "The very function of blessings over food . . . is the releasing of holy produce from the earth (which belongs to God) so that it is no longer holy, but profane and can thus be consumed by equally profane creatures (ourselves) living in a profane state."

26. Professor Rood recounted this event in a worship class at the Graduate Theological Union, Berkeley, c. 1997. At the end of the story, he pulled out two of these small brass communion cups, moving students to tears.

27. According to Turner, *instrumental symbols* have variable elements and "serve as means to the explicit or implicit goals of the given ritual." They are used to attain a goal in a particular ritual context. "Symbols in Ndembu Ritual," 45.

28. Turner calls *dominant symbols* "structural elements . . . which tend to be ends in themselves"; "Symbols . . . produce action, and dominant symbols tend to become focuses in interaction"; ibid., 45, 22. For Turner, dominant symbols have a meaning that they retain from rite to rite; ibid., 30–32.

29. "Diabolic" comes from *dia* and *ballein*, "to throw apart." That which lacks relationship and confuses meaning instead of mediating meaning, and separates rather than integrates, is the opposite of symbolic.

30. The other symbols of Christ's presence are the word proclaimed, as well as the two traditionally understood in the Roman church: the priest and the eucharistic elements of bread and wine. *Sacrosanctum Concilium* ("Constitution on the Sacred Liturgy"), in *The Documents of Vatican II* (New York: America, 1966), §7.

31. In classic rhetoric, the credibility and integrity of the leader/speaker is called the *ethos,* which is an essential part of the triad including the content of the rite or speech (*logos*) and the hearers' receipt

and response (*pathos*). See Lucy Lind Hogan, *Graceful Speech: An Invitation to Preaching* (Louisville: Westminster John Knox, 2006).

32. Louis-Marie Chauvet, *Symbol and Sacrament: A Sacramental Reinterpretation of Christian Existence* (Collegeville, MN: Liturgical, 1995), 330–46.

33. George Santayana is quoted in Clifford Geertz, "Religion as a Cultural System," in *The Interpretation of Cultures* (San Francisco: Basic, 1973), 87.

34. Paul Ricoeur addresses this aphorism in his concluding chapter in *The Symbolism of Evil* (Boston: Beacon, 1967), 347–57.

35. Susanne K. Langer, *Philosophy in a New Key: A Study in the Symbolism of Reason, Rite and Art*, 2d ed. (Cambridge: Harvard University Press, 1957 [1942]); see 19ff. "And the triumph of empiricism in science is jeopardized by the surprising truth that our sense-data are primarily symbols" (21).

36. Ibid., 24.

37. For example, see Jeanne M. Hoeft, *Agency, Culture and Human Personhood: Pastoral Theology and Intimate Partner Violence* (Eugene, Ore.: Pickwick, 2008).

38. For example, Carl Jung understands symbols also as distinct from signals (he calls them "signs"): "A sign is an analogous or abbreviated expression of a *known* thing. But a symbol is always the best possible expression of a relatively *unknown* fact, a fact, however, that is none the less recognized or postulated as existing." In *Psychological Types* (London: Routledge & Kegan Paul, 1949), 601.

39. Langer, *Philosophy in a New Key*, xiv (emphases hers).

40. Ibid., 26.

41. Paul Tillich, *Dynamics of Faith* (New York: Harper & Brothers, 1957), 41.

Chapter 4: Ritual Honesty

1. Elaine Ramshaw, *Ritual and Pastoral Care*, Theology and Pastoral Care (Philadelphia: Fortress Press, 1987), 26, passim.

2. Gordon W. Lathrop, *Holy Things: A Liturgical Theology* (Minneapolis: Fortress Press, 1993), 176.

3. For an excellent pastoral and theological discussion of the meaning and importance of lament as "bold, disturbing, and prophetic" but also honest and healing, see Kathleen D. Billman and Daniel L. Migliore, *Rachel's Cry: Prayer of Lament and Rebirth of Hope* (Cleveland: United Church Press, 1999), 2, 3. See also Walter Brueggemann's three chapters on exile and lament in Erskine Clarke, ed., *Exilic Preaching* (Harrisburg: Trinity Press International, 1998), 9–61.

4. Emily Dickinson, from her poem, "After great pain a formal feeling comes," in Thomas H. Johnson, ed., *Complete Poems of Emily Dickinson* (New York: Little, Brown, 1960), #341, v. 3.

5. Don Saliers, *Worship as Theology: Foretaste of Glory Divine* (Nashville: Abingdon, 1994), 21–38.

6. Lathrop, *Holy Things*, 176. The "major oppositions of the *ordo*" are called to "lively presence in the local assembly." Lathrop is speaking in the more specific context of Eucharist and baptism, for which the oppositions are "meeting and week, word and table, thanksgiving and beseeching, teaching and bath, *pascha* and year" (179).

7. "Center of value and power" is a term from James W. Fowler, *Stages of Faith: The Psychology of Human Development and the Quest for Meaning* (San Francisco: Harper & Row, 1981), 17, passim.

8. For clarification on the distinction, see the scientific studies of Hans Selye, including *Stress without Distress* (Philadelphia: Lippincott, 1974).

Chapter 5: Holy Sacrifice

1. Among Campbell's major works are *The Hero with a Thousand Faces* (Princeton: Princeton University Press, 1968), and his autobiography *The Hero's Journey: The World of Joseph Campbell,* ed. Phil Cousineau (San Francisco: Harper & Row, 1990).

2. This interpretation is confirmed in Robert J. Daly's critical book *Sacrifice Unveiled: The True Meaning of Christian Sacrifice* (New York: Continuum/T & T Clark, 2009). See also Daly's earlier work, including "The New Testament Concept of Christian Sacrificial Activity," *Biblical Theology Bulletin* 8 (1978): 99–107; *Christian Sacrifice: The Judeo-Christian Background before Origen* (Washington, DC: Catholic University of America Press, 1978); and "The Power of Sacrifice in Ancient Judaism and Christianity," *Journal of Ritual Studies* 4, no. 2 (1990): 181–98.

3. See James F. White, *Sacraments as God's Self-Giving* (Nashville: Abingdon, 1983).

4. Thomas Cranmer, *Book of Common Prayer*, 1549. See *The Two Liturgies, A.D. 1549, and A.D. 1552: with other Documents, set forth by authority in the Reign of King Edward the Sixth,* ed. for the Parker Society (Cambridge: Cambridge University Press, 1844), 89.

5. Augustine, from Sermon 227, quoted in Horton Davies, *Bread of Life and Cup of Joy: Newer Ecumenical Perspectives on the Eucharist* (Grand Rapids: Eerdmans, 1993), 127.

6. See Wendy Mogel, *The Blessing of a Skinned Knee: Using Jewish Teachings to Raise Self-Reliant Children* (New York: Scribner, 2001).

Chapter 6: The Paschal Mystery

1. On the call to lead people not to Christ per se, but to that to which *Christ* called people—namely the reign of God—see Mortimer Arias, *Announcing the Reign of God: Evangelization and the Subversive Memory of Jesus* (Philadelphia: Fortress Press, 1984).

2. Ronald Rolheiser, *The Holy Longing: The Search for a Christian Spirituality* (New York: Doubleday, 1999), 146.

3. Ibid., 145.

4. Ibid., esp. chap. 7, 141–66.

5. Ibid., 141.

6. Ibid., 146.

7. Ibid.

8. Ibid.

9. Ibid., 147.

10. Ibid., 148.

11. Ibid., 148–62.

12. Ibid., 165.

13. See Pamela Cooper-White, *Shared Wisdom: Use of the Self in Pastoral Care and Counseling* (Minneapolis: Fortress Press, 2004). She describes the need for empathy and for offering its insights to the focal persons for *them* to claim or not claim.

14. Tad Guzie, *The Book of Sacramental Basics* (Mahwah, NJ: Paulist, 1981). According to Guzie, the "rhythm that makes life human" includes lived (meaningful, reflected-upon) experience, story, and festivity.

15. Corrie Ten Boom with John and Elizabeth Sherrill, *The Hiding Place* (Washington Depot, CT: Chosen, 1971).

16. *Baptism, Eucharist and Ministry,* Faith and Order Paper #111 (Geneva: World Council of Churches, 1982), "Baptism" II.A.§3.

17. The Rt. Rev. Theodore Eastman in a 1984 presentation in Anchorage, Alaska, made the point that *every* sacrament includes death and resurrection: death to one reality and birth to another. See also his *The Baptizing Community: Christian Initiation and the Local Congregation* (New York: Seabury, 1982).

18. Jim Clarke draws a distinction between *ceremony* and *ritual.* In his language, high school graduation is a ceremony because it does not have the transformative valence of a ritual. See his *Creating Rituals: A New Way of Healing for Everyday Life* (Mahwah, NJ: Paulist, 2011). While I do not distinguish the terms as discretely as Clarke, I think it essential that Christians understand the paschal mystery to be what operates transformationally. For the theoretical background to the current work, see my dissertation, *Christian Ritualizing and the Baptismal Process: Liturgical Explorations toward a Realized Baptismal Ecclesiology* (Eugene, OR: Wipf & Stock, 2012).

19. See Mary Catherine Hilkert, *Naming Grace: Preaching and the Sacramental Imagination* (New York: Continuum, 2002).

20. See Catherine Pickstock, *After Writing: On the Liturgical Consummation of Philosophy* (Oxford: Blackwell, 1998).

Index

acting on behalf of. *See* speaking/acting on behalf of
adelphopoiesis, 35, 141n19
Anderson, Herbert, 19, 139n2, 140n25, 140n1, 142n20
Anderson, Megory, 40–41, 141n25, 141n27
Augustine, 116, 146n5
Aune, Michael, viii, 139n2, 141n12

baptism
    ministry of. *See* ministry of the baptized
    process of, 15, 34, 39, 65, 124, 125, 129, 131, 141n18, 146n18
    rite of renewal of, 31
Baptism, Eucharist, Ministry (ecumenical document), 28
Bell, Catherine, viii, 4–9, 13, 30, 39, 55, 56, 74, 139n3, 139n4, 139n6
Bourdieu, Pierre, 62, 139n8
Bouwsma, William, 9, 139n13

Campbell, Joseph, 110, 145n1
Chauvet, Louis-Marie, 62, 84, 139n5, 143n23, 145n32
Christendom, 21, 140n19
    post-Christendom, 9, 86, 123

competence, symbolic, 76–77
creativity. *See also* play
    as arising in tension, 103, 106, 137
    in ritual makers, 19, 36–37, 43–44, 61, 111, 133, 135, 137

Education for Ministry (Bible study program), 143n9. *See also* metaphor, entering the world of
effectiveness
    experiential, 28–29, 33, 43, 50, 91, 141n12
    theological, 28–29, 30, 32–33, 35, 37, 50, 112, 141n12
efficacy, operational. *See* effectiveness, experiential
empathy, 23, 27, 36–41, 44, 63–64, 71, 109, 132, 141n20, 146n13
ethics
    as attribute of rite makers, 46–49, 51, 63, 89
    and Christian life, 35, 49, 60–61, 71, 102
    and emotional honesty, 99; see also honesty, ritual
    of liturgy and ritual, 4, 13, 14, 19, 51, 89, 142n7